Muse Mysteria

Book One: Invocation

by J. Wells Kara

Mythos Publishing

MYTHOS
Publishing

Muses Mysteria
Book One: Invocation
By J. Wells Kara

ISBN: 979-8-218-75002-2
Library of Congress Control Number: 2025907093

Consulting Editor: Cheri M. Hyde
Cover Design: J. Wells Kara
Interior Design: Mythos Publishing
First Edition Hardcover, May 2025
Book Website: www.jwellskara.com

Disclaimer:
The author and publisher have made every effort to ensure the accuracy and completeness of the information in this book. However, it is not intended to diagnose or treat any medical or psychological condition. Readers should consult their own medical professionals for health concerns. The author, publisher, and affiliates disclaim any liability or risk arising from the use of this content.

This book may include speculative, or mythopoetic portrayals of historical, religious, or mythological figures. These depictions are not intended as literal representations of real individuals, living or deceased, but as creative interpretations within a literary context. No guarantees are made regarding the accuracy or reliability of the information, which is provided "as is" and may reflect symbolic, or imaginative perspectives based on limited or disputed historical data.

Dedicated to life, love, my mentors, the Muses, the Divine, my ancestors and descendants, and all those who have supported me along this wondrous and magical path.

Contents

"We are servants of the Mystery. We were put here on earth to act as agents of the Infinite, to bring into existence that which is not yet, but which will be, through us. Every breath we take, every heartbeat, every evolution of every cell comes from God [Goddess] and is sustained by God [Goddess] every second, just as every creation, invention, every bar of music or line of verse, every thought, vision, fantasy, every dumb-ass flop and stroke of genius comes from that infinite intelligence that created us and the universe in all its dimensions, out of the Void, the field of infinite potential, primal chaos, the Muse. To acknowledge that reality, to efface all ego, to let the work come through us and give it back freely to its source, that, in my opinion, is as true to reality as it gets."

—Steven Pressfield, *The War of Art*
(with insertion)

Preface

This path is an invitation to embrace the Mystery of the Muse as a source of healing, creation, and inspiration. Their Mysteries beckon us to expand and rediscover the inner realm of ourselves. The Muse has arrived to awaken and pour the sacred waters of the Divine Feminine back into the dry, cracked rivers of the psyche and the living Earth. Their offering dives into the creative self through stories, the dreamworld, and myth.

As the world undergoes breakdown and degradation, we invite possibilities for ourselves and the changing culture. Amid the pandemic, I watched the world fall to its knees. Next, political and economic storms began to brew. Bewildered, confused, and heartbroken, I pushed open the gate of mystery. Why are these crises appearing at our door? I received no answer. Instead, several ancient Greek goddesses of power emerged, hovering above chaos and ruin. Gathered by a sacred well with vibrant lifeforce, its waters teeming with potential.

These Nine Greek Goddesses, the Muses, revealed their mission to guide us in reimagining and igniting a creative rebirth. This is part of their work and love, transforming a reckoning into the extraordinary. They encourage and activate our imaginations to run wild across fields and into unknown places.

They provide us with hope, which feeds humanity with the strength to create the new. This, stirred with action, intention, and love, can transform worlds. At this pivotal moment, our collective stands at a crossroads. We can either persist in a path that harms life or break through to a future beyond our wildest dreams. One that nurtures all beings. With the Muse by our side, we enter enchantment, ritual, and storytelling.

The Muses are ready to ignite and elate us on our journey through their mysteries. As we face this monumental wave of change, I raise the torch of illumination, vision, and hope in my right hand, while in my left, I hold the chalice of the heart, overflowing with creation.

Introduction

The Muse spoke from within: It is time to re-enter life and create with the world.

Some urge has edged you toward these inner workings. Perhaps your inner Muse is calling. It might be the fire from your creative self asking you to awaken, stretch, and travel beyond the comfortable known. Or the currents of the Mysteries summoned you to explore the depths of your soul. Whatever the reason, you are at this juncture of life.

The calling of the Muse is one way to participate, transform, and rebirth ourselves. You are giving over a part of your life to mystery. For most in our modern society, going through an initiation or rite of passage into the mysteries can feel overwhelming. A person can easily find themselves tumbling through the transitional turbulence because most of these teachings have been lost, hidden, or negated.

By surrendering a part of your life to the unknown, you enter into a space where the things that have held you back are revealed. Shifting one's gaze inward to the senses, patterns, and habits is an opportunity to discern what to keep or shed. Working alongside the Muse not only transforms you—it also ripples outward, benefiting the collective on a profound scale.

It is by no accident that for the last twenty-five years, we have witnessed many going through a dark night of the soul and self-realization. A dark night is a rite of passage through the underworld and abyss. It usually asks us to give up our previous lives, stripping us of every aspect of what we once knew. Many have had to find their way through alone. We are fortunate to live in a time when these happenings have been documented. Many who have gone through such spiritual experiences are helping others along the way. But what comes after? How does one move back into the world and integrate. Who are the midwives standing at the threshold of our return from dark nights or after loss and destruction? Who helps us create a new life? After all, Demeter stands at the gate to welcome Persephone's emergence each spring. It's not that we require a mother figure, but there was someone to guide her home because it *is* a transition.

Few texts explore the rite of rebirth or the integration that follows the long voyage back into life. More often, we are left to midwife ourselves into a society still caught in friction and illusion. At the threshold of the abyss, in the first contractions of returning, we begin to carry with us the deeper inner world we've encountered and, from it, build anew. I don't claim this is the only way—it's one way. The Muses remind us that the Creative Spirit can bridge the divide and midwife us into our becoming and rebirth.

Structure of the Book

Muse Mysteria was guided by the Muse and embodies their essence and frequency. Most of the information was gathered in a trance-like state and through conscious channeling. Through this process, I discovered that each Muse transmitted their messages differently. Some were more visual, while others used words. Occasionally, people would enter my life with an energy similar to the Muse I worked with. I would stumble upon books, movies, or passages that resonated with me. This is often typical of how mystery unfolds in the outer world.

While it is fascinating to romanticize and reminisce about the past and explore key authors of history and antiquity, we can not fully comprehend what life was like through the lens of the ancient world. The filter of present-day experiences and worldviews will inevitably influence how someone interprets the past. You may have encountered this a few times if you enjoy peering into history. Having said that, I have done that on occasion throughout this book from the perspective of a mystic and trained Priestess because there is not enough information or accounts of the Muses except for a few storytellers in history, who will be briefly introduced.

Stepping out of the imaginary box, I purposely capitalized words out of respect and honor for particular energies. For instance, Deity, Underworld, Void, Nymphs, etcetera, are not typos. The ancient Greek author Hesiod similarly wrote these capitulations in his poem *Theogony*. The ancient Greeks did not use indentations, line breaks, or spaces between words, sentences, or paragraphs. I've added spaces for clarity, as inspired by the Muse's desired style.

We begin the book with the cosmology of ancient Greece and explore the stories and lives of each Muse. In Part One of *Muse Mysteria*, we start with the origins of the Muses in early Greek civilization during the Geometric Period (circa 900–700 BCE) and continue into Archaic Greece (circa 700–480 BCE). Connecting with the original threads of stories and myths is essential to understanding where we have come from and the direction in which we are heading, with the caveat that we can shift and change.

Part two, *Muse Self-Initiation*, is a venture through each Muse, with storytelling, journeys, and well-wishes. The final chapter concludes with a choice of how you would like to continue working with the Muses.

Initiation

I'd like to mention initiations, a topic often debated. While there are many perspectives on whether self-initiation is a valid approach, I believe it is as valid as any other form of initiation.

Rather than an external guide, tradition, or teacher, you become your own initiator, discovering your path through a personal connection, like in this book, with the Muses and their Mysteries. An initiation with an elder or tradition is often designed to provide protection, accountability, guidance—especially for pitfalls along the way, and a good dose of ego-dismantling.

Another form is cohort initiation, where a group of individuals comes together to initiate themselves collectively. In a shared container, each person holds space and offers mutual accountability. This kind of initiation requires an understanding of shadow work, the willingness to give one another room to make mistakes, and the ability to allow each person's journey to unfold in its own time without force or judgment.

A fourth type of initiation is one that comes directly through Spirit. It is often far more tumultuous, destabilizing, and challenging, as it leads to ego annihilation—though some sense of self does eventually resurface. I won't be exploring this type of initiation in this book, but it's certainly a potent topic.

In self-initiation, the one holding you accountable is *yourself*. When you surrender to your practice and dedication, it can be as powerful as any external rite. It becomes a crucible of transformation and a space where you learn, discern, and cultivate inner authority. Having said that, you may do a hybrid-initiation and seek support from a mentor, therapist, or guide to help you navigate challenges or offer feedback. The helper might be with you for part of the journey or full-time. Ultimately, the path is yours to walk. Self-initiation is the act of taking the first step on your own magical and creative life.

This book is a pathwork. You will be guided through stories and journeys; the process is yours to shape. The framework offered here is a foundation to help you explore your unique relationship with the Muse, allowing you to work in a way that feels authentic and true to you. If you're more advanced, you may be drawn to creating your own rituals, performances, or aspecting. All of these can be powerful expressions of transformation and magic.

As you begin this journey, I encourage you to read each chapter sequentially. Each Muse leads you into the next as the path unfolds. If you feel led, consider reading through one Muse per month. This will deepen your connection with their energy. In the same light, you can form small groups to amplify the experience. Working from new moon to new moon encourages growth, visioning, and empowerment.

I suggest keeping a journal for how each Muse shows up for you. You may notice things around you shift, and people might show up with similar attributes. By nature, you will be drawn to some Muses more than others. Note that the one who challenges you may hold your greatest gift.

If possible, avoid any recreational substances (if you are taking prescription drugs or supplements, please continue as directed by your doctor) when reading or journeying, as they can impede the development of the magical muscle and the ability to hold energy for oneself. We are capable of getting into elevated states without the use of recreational substances.

The deeper you immerse yourself in the Muse, the more profound your magical activation will become. May your path be smooth and your journey flourish with life and creativity.

Mending the Threads

The stories of the Muses about the Muses are theirs to tell. The stories they chose to communicate are what we need in our current culture and worldview. Imagine them storytelling with you by a fire or performing vignettes, energetically sparking aliveness within you. They hold parts of truth to the process of rebirth and the journey of the creative self.

Their stories, poems, and well-wishes hold a new thread for us. We have been told that we are the result of a broken culture from long ago. Even though things may have been broken, they are not lost. Wisdom and nature always find their way through cracks and barren places.

With their creative hands, the Muses are tying a new thread to the old frayed one, mending them together, strengthening and fortifying them with golden threads. Things will never be as they once were, but the supportive energy and wisdom will find their place and way to stream back into the world.

With well-wishes,
J. Wells Kara

Invocation

Great Muses of Ancestry
Nine wonders of poetry, song, and art
Goddesses born from Thunder and Memory
I call out to you in this time of illusion
From the mist of wars, destruction, separation, and injustices
I invoke thee!

Bestow on this work and to humanity
your loving grace, inspiration, and healing
Let your wells and hymns once again wash
over and heal our distressed psyches with ease

Grant us your sight, song, poetry, dance, and humor
Steer us to an era of love, creativity, connection,
and to wholeness

Bless our minds; these hearts
and hands as we reimagine
a new way forward

May this work breathe life back into the world
so all will flourish and thrive
with fecundity and life

May the content and magic of this work
be guided by your inspiration, protection, and love
May this work move through all the worlds
in the best way possible for all Beings
and our descendants

PART I

Muse Mysteria

Prelude

In the Beginning, There Were Three

At first, it was quiet. Silent. Not even a breath. A dark Void. Empty. One. Limitless, yet complete.

Then, a great sound struck! A note sprang forth, and then two. What followed was a cacophony of Chaos. Here and then there, great energy unfolds faster, with movement, potential, and flashpoint.

Shifting, stretching, turning, opening, whole beings began to emerge at an enormous speed. Great primordial forces lit up the entire cosmos. Gaea and the whole sky spun and danced, Ouranus of the Heavens, Kronos, Eros, Oceanus, twelve in all. Giant beings, immortals named Titans, are the predecessors of the Olympians. The Elder Gods were born.

Before long, a song was heard at the birth of three. Gaea and Ouranus, conceived three Titan daughters. Melete, Aoede, and Mneme are the first of the Muse line.

Melete was the firstborn and the gift of practice itself. She resides in meditation, focus, and inward knowing. Aoede, the Muse of voice, instrument, and song. Mneme, memory, her poem awakening, remembrance, and lost wisdom followed. She went on to give birth to the Nine Muses.

They sent forth harmony, art, and inspiration to Gaea. It landed in humans and rested in their Psyche. Now, ice turned to fire, mountains grew and climbed, and landscapes shifted. Flora, then fauna, thrived. The Moon called to the Oceans.

Soon, the Creative Spirits and sacred fire took hold of the mortals. The Muses' hands began guiding, shifting, and shaping the world. Civilizations were created. Craft, skill, and art began to flourish…

Chapter I
The Fated Birth of Myth

Every story, in one way or another, starts with a Muse...

NINE WOMEN GRACEFULLY STEPPED CLOSER IN SIMILAR POSES AND STRIDES. *With delicate hands and strong stances, their gazes met the rising sun. In a united chant, they sang the return of the day, the body, and the senses. A thunderous drumming echoed from the heart of the great mountain. An electric sound erupted from below their feet and rushed over their beings, their fingers, and their lyres. There, a mile above the waters and crashing tides, their singing beckoned Hesiod forth.*

On the fertile ground of Mount Helikon, flowers sprouted from each footstep. Hearing these Divine Beings' songs, Hesiod felt compelled to ascend the mountain to accept his fate. Kneeling before Muse, with his head bowed in reverence, the world fell loudly silent, and the air calmed.

Calliope, the eldest of the Muses, spoke softly, "Hesiod, rise and meet your Fate." He stood up and stepped forward in his elated state. An illuminated staff of laurel was extended to him. Her melodious and enchanting voice pierced him with the words of truth. Hesiod accepted this gift and responsibility as he took hold of the staff, along with it, the vow.

Once he declared his promise, Calliope peered within him, lifted her arms, and sang to the sky. A great wind blew forth, and the breath of the Divine Voice merged within him. Seized by this great power, he struggled and braced himself upon the Earth. "Go and sing of the Gods and the immortals of creation," Calliope said. *She turned and walked toward the sacred well with her sisters and disappeared.*

Hesiod awakened and felt a change deep within him. With eyes filled with tears flowing anew, words descended onto papyrus in long waves as his hands wrote of the Gods and unprecedented everyday tales. Hesiod offered Theogony, a poem, as promised to the Muses. Walking into the theater arena, he centered himself. With all the power within his being, he began to sing and invoke Zeus's nine daughters by name.

Klio the Proclaimer, Melpomene of Tragedy, Erato of Erotic Poetry, Euterpe of Song, Terpsichore of Dance, Thalia of Comedy, Polyhymnia of Sacred Hymns, Calliope of Epic Poetry, and Urania of Astronomy.

Pronounced for the first time from his lips, the names passed over the crowd and rained into the hearts of all who watched. For those called by the Muse, by the creative lifeforce, by Spirit, a great momentum exists toward the flame of the soul. Ancient peoples across many cultures knew and understood the gifts of the Divine spark.

I am Mneme, Mother of Muses and Keeper of Myth and Memory

In the ancient folds of the imagination, before words met ink, I held the past myths soon to be. I breathed the first stories into the world, which passed from ear to ear and heart to heart. Long before the written word became the pages of history, tales lived within the currents of the creative realm. Tales which danced upon the words of orators, passing through the magic of the Gods and the voices of mortals. I bring you this epic from the realms of Greece, long ago, with the story of a farmer from the mountain of myths on Helikon.

At this point, humanity awakens to a time when mortals begin to shape their voices. This is where the dreamers, the seers, and the storytellers gave life to what was once lived in the imagination, a journey long before you were born.

I speak first of Hesiod, the one who captured the whispers of the Divine in verse. He conceived the poem *Theogony* to fulfill a vow to my daughters, the nine Muses. He pledged to sing, name, and record the origin of the Gods and Goddesses, surrendering his voice to the pulse of creation. In return for his devotion, he was blessed with the sacred gift of the Poet's voice, which would echo through the ages.

As Hesiod relayed, there were only three Muses in the beginning: myself and my two sisters. And so, nine new Muses were born from my flowering of life. Alongside this birth, the swelling of human vision and the arrival of emerging dreams and stories. You see, a wondrous mosaic of change was occurring.

My daughters opened the world's heart, and new roles were forged in the stirring of culture. Their chorus of transformation spread like a flame across the land, and the ways of civilization rapidly shifted. Agriculture and economics blossomed, as did the myths, stories, rituals, and arts. Their influence flowed through the lives of those who dared to speak, create, and know.

Hesiod set the stage for our presence in the world with his written words. Yet, let me tell you two other origin stories of the Muses, born of their own time and place in central Greece. One story is from the peaks of Mount Olympus, where I met the God of Thunder, Zeus. The second tale speaks of Pegasus, whose mighty wings could carry the heavens.

Nine Amazing Nights on Mount Olympus

With her footprints behind her in the burning sand
she did not look back
Trusting the prophecy and the winds to move her forward

Tears of what came before
fell to dry Earth
At this moment, she did not know she would be awakening to Love

After years of conflict, the Titanomachy war spun on
Mneme already knew the fate and ending of Titans and Olympians
For memory reminds that which has been forgotten
to never repeat
she knew of the forgetfulness of both Gods and mortals

Her gaze turned up at the blazing sun
clouds in the distance began to form
A nebula of mist swirled
white to blue, shifting into purple as the sky rumbled

Light rippled, danced, and branched across the horizon
before long, drops of rain and forceful gales
She steadied herself
a barrage of cracking and crashing gave way to thunderbolts

Before her, between clouds, she saw
a radiant God born of Earth and Time
Their eyes met, the Olympian raised a hand of thunder

The Titan, Mneme
softly approaches, showing memory has no quarrels
she knew the revelation to be fulfilled

A gust swiftly enamored Mneme
carrying her north a great distance
Gently reaching Mount Olympus,
she met with the Olympian counsel

For She held the prophecy of the Fates
those who recited the mysteries
And that which is yet to be
Mneme heard the words again

—A tide of change will pour over the Earth
The first twelve of power will give birth
and fall to the second

In the days ahead, Mneme connected closer with Zeus
both developing a passion of similar outcome
Now, no distance between the primordial Cosmos and Earthly Deity
in sacred union, an embrace of memory and lightning
converging in one breath, an illuminating ecstatic elation

The nights passed; one became two, then three
On the ninth night, but before the first light of the tenth
nine daughters in all were born
Over each of these nights, a Muse
singing the song of their own name

Klio of Times Past, Melpomene of Tragedy, Erato of Desire, Euterpe of
Song, Terpsichore of Dance, Thalia of Comedy, Polyhymnia of Sacred
Hymns, Calliope of Epic Poetry and Urania of Astronomy.

Mneme tenderly held her daughters and enchanted each with memory
prophecy, creativity, and eloquence
to ensure humanity never forgets

As Mneme, my story has continued to morph and shift throughout time and land

We, the Titans, are at the beginning of the Greek creation story. We, the tall, magic-wielding primordials, were pushed out of power by the Olympians after a ten-year war. This was a tough time for both Gods and mortals. We all struggled with the polarization and separation taking place. My daughters, the Nine Muses, are the third generation from the inception of Chaos, the Void, Gaea, and Eros. Gaea, the Earth, is their grandmother. That connection runs deep.

In my sacred union with Zeus, the great awakener, a bond transcending mere symbolism held us. Combining the electric nature of thunder and the power of memory points to the path of self-realization. One must consider their perspective to grasp my words. Remember, "*Know Thyself*" (or *Gnothi Seauton*, in Greek), the ancient wisdom inscribed at the entrance of the Temple of the Oracle of Delphi, serves as a guiding light. The Greeks revered the essence of memory. The rhapsodies sang, and philosophers understood the importance of remembering. We, the Muses, help ensure the lessons of the past endure and are recognized by the collective consciousness.

Today, you view things with defined edges, categories, and no gray areas. But the Divine Feminine energies don't fit nicely into any box and never will. By far, we are the most ephemeral and fluid in nature out of the entire pantheon of Gods and Goddesses. We are part of the essential lifeforce and reside energetically to work and guide through you. We provide the movement in areas of creative expression: love, tragedy, humor, dance, the past, story, music, sacred words, the stars, the future, and prophecy. Our inspiration is a call to action. When you feel the divine spark igniting in your depths, you are opening and embracing the moment. This is a place of great power.

Pegasus on Helikon

In the quiet vastness of the heavens,
where stars shimmer, and dreams take flight,
Pegasus, the winged one, awoke

From a great song
reaching out across the sky and the stars, a call.
Beyond, a majestic Being awakened

He listened, shook, and spread his wings
leaping forward, he made way into a quickening gallop

Over clouds and through thunder
this celestial stallion hastened.
Born from the Great Protector Medusa
and the mighty God of the Sea

Moving closer to the chant, he glanced below
at Mount Helikon.
From the power of words and aria
the mountain ascended, climbed, and clambered

With tremendous force and a great leap
Pegasus galloped and hooved the ground on Mount Helikon
ceasing the quaking summit
Below, springing forth from two of the marked impressions
water poured

With it, a pulsating light spread over the mountain
across the land and touched the singing Bard beneath
The influence toppled the Poet
who dropped to the ground, releasing the song

In a moment, another resounding voice was heard
Far above, flowing from the wellspring Hippocrene
a sweet, Divine melody

The Poet noted nine magnificent Beings appearing
around the spring's cusp
Struck with inspiration, the Bard sang an offering

Pegasus, circling back over Helikon
glided softly toward the spring
He greeted the Muses of art, poetry, song, and story

From this day forth, wells, springs, and streams
were enchanted with inspiration
for whoever drank from them

There are several tales about how many marked impressions emerged upon the summit

Some stories speak of two impressions, while others, the more ancient ones, speak of four. From these impressions, two names appeared. One is called Aganippe, an aspect of the great Goddess Demeter, whose blessings nourished the land. The other is Hippocrene, the fabled spring from which my daughters appeared, their voices rising from its waters. These waters are still upon the slopes of Mount Helikon and flow in your time. Many who find the well and drink from it are said to become blessed with the Poetic Voice.

Pegasus is the guardian of fresh waters, springs, and wells. Across the ancient world, many held the elements sacred and revered; these forces shaped the world's soul. And water, well, it was seen as the most receptive of all the elements, a conduit of life. The Muse flows with water, carrying their stories on its currents. When my daughters and I traveled, we found offerings of food, song, and art left in the hope we would grant the creative spark.

I have spoken enough of the past. Now, let us turn to the future and to the Mysteries...

Chapter II
What Came Before

"The past is the teacher of the present." —Greek Proverb

B*EFORE HER THE SACRED DOOR TO THE MYSTERIES. Reaching into her pocket, she retrieved the golden key. How many lives did it take to arrive at this place? Few have entered, not because it was forbidden, but because it was forgotten. The ancestors tucked it away thousands of years ago for safekeeping.*

Beneath the full moon's glow at the entrance, I traced the ancient patterns etched into the door. Memories flooded back. A copper coin my mother had given me, loss, a trip to Rome, and a call for something more. All of which unknowingly set my life into motion.

"I miss you," I whispered, wiping my tears. "Guide me back to my words and life." I tossed the copper coin, watching it vault high and spin. For a moment, time slowed, the wind stirred, and chimes rang. The coin shined in the moonlight as it plunged into the fountain at Tempio di Esculapio. Ripples spiraled outward across the waters of the God of Healing.

A somber silence settled over me as I circled back to the hotel on Abruzzi Road. It was hard to believe my parents had been gone for two years. Rome had been the last place they wanted to visit prior to the accident. In a way, this trip was honoring them.

I checked my phone. There were several emails; One was an invitation to a curated lecture on *'The Art of Letter Writing During the Early Renaissance'* at the National Roman Museum, which I deleted, and two from my friend

Jenna, who had just married and bought a home. Ignoring the messages, I returned to my room. On the floor was an envelope; someone must have pushed it underneath the door. It was another invite to the National Roman Museum; it read:

Dear Grace C. Bellas,

You are invited to attend our Biannual Art & Literature: Through the Ages, featuring 'The Art of Letter Writing During the Early Renaissance' tomorrow at 18:00 di sera.

I tore up the invitation, tossed it in the recycle bin, and hurried to dinner across the street. Outside my hotel room the next day, yet another invite lay on the floor. 'Did you get an invitation to a lecture tonight?' Asking the woman in the hall.

"No." The woman said.

I placed it in my bag and dashed outside the door for an espresso and to visit the Colosseum until...

"Grace?" A woman in a stunning long blue dress, sunglasses, and matching wide-brimmed hat held out an invitation.

"Yes?"

"This is for you. If you head that way now, you'll make it to the lecture," she pointed. "You don't want to be late."

"I took the envelope and watched her saunter off, curious if she was giving invitations to anyone else. I looked around the Colosseum and asked, 'Did you get one of these?' The group of women shook their heads. *What is happening right now?* I wondered, curiosity bubbling up.

Arriving at the museum, it was empty. Double-checking the information; it was accurate. Sigh. I took a sip of water and checked the hall. "Was that there before?" An event sign featuring a dancing Muse was displayed near another exhibit.

Lecture tour: Mysteries of the Muses: Discovering Muse Relics from Ancient Greek Settlements, with Dr. Sophia M. Kyrios. 18.00 di sera.

I wandered in and joined the group circled around an ancient Greek statue. The detail and realism of each figure were powerful—frozen expressions in time.

"This evening, we will tour the recent Muse relics uncovered in Greece and how they made their way to Rome in the 3rd century," said Dr. Kyrios. In her early 50s, Dr. Kyrios was a renowned academic and historian. She seemed familiar. Two seamless hours slipped by as we wandered through the exhibit. I was about to leave when her words caught my attention.

"The Muses are alive today. If you listen closely, you might hear them calling to awaken your gifts," said Dr. Kyrios. At the end of the tour, she gathered her notes and spoke to a few from our group.

"Are you saying we all carry the Muse within us? Anyone can call on them?" I asked.

"Yes, you could put it that way, though it's not guaranteed. It requires study, curiosity, and dedication, which are rare nowadays. Most people are only drawn to those distracting digital devices."

"I'm curious and interested in the Muses."

She stopped, noticing the conviction in my voice. "I know someone in Greece. Hand me your phone. Her name is Ella, and she's in Athens. If you're serious and ready, you'll find her there."

Three days later, I headed for Athens. As I settled into the hotel room, there was a soft knock at the door. When I opened the door, I found an envelope on the floor. I glanced both ways down the hallway, then carefully tore open the side. A golden key slipped out and fell to the floor. Just then, my phone chimed—it was a text from Ella with instructions and the meeting place.

*Dear Initiate, here is what you need to know to prepare
for what is ahead…*

The Uber driver stopped about twenty minutes southeast of Athens, in front of a black metal gate.

"Are you sure this is the place, miss? Do you want me to wait?" His voice was raspy and concerned.

"This is the place," I assured him, stepping out of the car.

Walking past the gate and up the pathway, a wave of uncertainty spread through my body. *Is this a good idea?*

At the other end of the bend stood another gate and a set of ornate double doors. A gust of wind rustled the leaves, and the hoot of an owl added to the power of the moment. Placing the key in the lock, I took a deep breath and turned it. A sharp ringing vibrated and split the atmosphere around me. The patterns on the door shifted as light changed into indescribable colors. This radiant illumination spread across the entryway, beneath my feet, and soared upward into the night. As the entrance shifted open, the atmosphere changed. The fragrance of rose and myrrh poured forth. Beyond the threshold was a captivating woman in a simple, flowing robe. Her intense, focused eyes locked with mine, as if she could see into my depths.

"I am Ella, the Wayfinder of the Hall. Inside is the Muse Mysteria, a journey into the depths of Mystery. It is a passage through the veil. How will you enter?"

"As Initiate," I said.

"Know you enter by your own free will and accord. You are accountable for your actions and choices and hold the key to your journey. I'm simply a guide and ally."

"I accept."

She moved closer and placed her hand on my head. "Enter, initiate," she said.

I took each step with intention across the threshold. Another robed Priestess greeted me with an antique bronze censer billowing with smoke. She carefully moved around my body, then waved for me to continue. Inside the next room, a sacred natural spring flowed. Torches cast an ethereal glow, and as mist swirled around me, thickening the air. My senses opened as the space expanded. The green marble floor was cool beneath my feet, its surface smooth and soothing.

"It's custom to purify before meeting the Muse," Ella said as she left.

I sank into the bubbling warm water, expanding my awareness inward as my muscles relaxed. A low hum vibrated every corner of the room, and I could feel the weight of my anxieties begin to fade.

After a time, I gradually opened my eyes and sensed that the purification had finished. Treading out of the pool, I reached for the soft garment set aside, wrapped it around me, and left my old clothes behind. There was a lightness to my body and clarity of mind. My eyes shifted toward the far side of the room. I knocked, and the door opened. Ella appeared and gestured for me to follow.

A vast corridor was lined with thresholds. Light filtered from stars, illuminating ancient trees along the walls. She guided me to a set of majestic wooden doors, carved and decorated with hues of blue.

"You must knock and enter yourself," she said.

"Which Muse is on the other side?"

"You will have to find out," said Ella.

I hesitated, then knocked, turned the handle, and ventured inward. Another world appeared before me as a large amphitheater constructed of stone, soil, and timber. Beyond the semicircle stretched waterfalls, rolling hills, and a lush emerald forest. In the center of the room, two chairs stood within a ring of water. As I made my way to the center, my pulse raced in anticipation of the Muse's arrival. There were so many questions to ask her. While eagerly waiting, I noticed two women singing, their melodious voices drifting from the northern end of the space. A divine presence materialized, gliding gracefully down the stairs. When the Muse and her guides reached the center of the room, I felt awkward. How does one properly greet a Muse? With a deep bow, I paused. The Muse smiled tenderly. Without saying a word, she seated herself, and her guides silently departed.

"I am Klio," she said. As the Muse of all things Past, I already know who you are. You think you know the truth to this answer, but you will live it before you leave your journey. You were summoned to the Muse Mysteria by the call of your soul. The golden key is not a happenstance; it is to introduce you to the Mysteries and what has come before. We have plenty to cover. If you are ready, we will begin."

I watched Klio pull out an ancient book, a cover worn by time, and place it on her lap. "Even though my memory is impeccable, it is helpful to create a backdrop for the story," she said, her eyes sparkling. Kilo opened the book. "Let's begin with the history and connection between the Muses, mortals, and Gods. A time when the ancient Mysteries once thrived. An approach to life that threaded and trickled through 11,000 years across present-day Greece, Egypt, Iran, Italy, and Türkiye.

These four Mystery traditions, which I will briefly describe, developed and provided a space and a way to complete these passages. The Mystagogues were aware of society's influences and limiting beliefs. Depending on the mystery journey and the individual's readiness, ordinary reality would disappear, revealing a path and purpose. These rites served as remedies, renewing the self or guiding one to the next life.

Initiate, you see, the oldest story is about birth, life, and death, and through it all, one powerful constant—love.

As Muse, we inspire life as art. You are the creator of your existence, a gift from Gaea herself; your body is a part of her essence. Each day, you craft a song, a poem, a story of your life, an epic journey from first breath to last. To navigate these stories, myths, and rites of passage were formed to guide you through life's transitions.

You will not need to take any notes. Instead, let these stories wash over you, and their Mysteries enter you. Let them integrate into your being. Breathe them in and feel their aliveness. These poems convey wisdom traditions thousands of years old."

From Sacred Gate to Eleusinian Mysteries

With torches in hand, pilgrims greeted the night
toward the setting sun
Thousands journeyed in procession of song
in-between green hills along the valley

Elefsina was met, where they purified
their bodies and souls
In the distance, across the water,
fires lit with Mysteries

Guided by those who walked before,
pointing the Sacred Way
They chanted the rise of the Goddess
as Initiates drank kykeon and wine

Arriving from the Underworld,
Winter's departure turns to Spring's renewal
Singing the story of Demeter and Persephone,
sacred dramas were enacted, and drums erupted

With sacred stories at Eleusis, on the final day
the Hierophant raised a torch and voice...
proclaiming Persephone's return and rebirth,
to keep the Earth and fields alive once more.

Isis, Mother of Mystery

In October's ritual of sorrow
with the Mother of Mystery
a precession gave way to
purification

Holding the vessel of the Nile
Priestesses poured water over
Initiates, washing their psyches
as they entered the sanctum

Wearing a simple white linen
the speaker of incantations
echoed Eleusinian Mysteries
a journey through the Underworld
began

Sun, Moon, and Stars were Guides
inside the inner temple
each novice searching for self
those lost aspects found and
transformed

The Bringer of magic assisted
a cathartic mourning and release
Love replacing fear
of the unknown and death

Initiates in the afterlife
with sigil promised salvation
to live again once more in this life
in Wholeness and Being.

Samothracian – Greater God's Mysteries

From the Cosmos and Constellations
lived the Greater Gods
Twins born of magic lived with the Pelagians
on the Island of Samothrace

From boat, few stepped upon this shore
of the Aegean Sea
They ventured toward the sacred river
where another Mysteria awaited

At daybreak, they entered
hearing the sounds of songs and drums
Ecstatic dancers attuned to
the stories handed down before religion

From the stoa, blindfolded Initiates
whispered confessions
Journeyed with Hekate, Hermes, and Nike
and heroes who came before

From Hekate's cave, they found
release and purpose
And travelled through the Underworld
back into this existence

From the theater, they witnessed
the sacred drama of marriage
Harmonia and Camdus
poured their wine over altar stones

In the hall, Initiates made offerings
to guarantee guidance
Protection by sea
with prayer, with symbols, with love

A golden ring and talismans
mark the end of their ordeal
Casting spiritual protection
from the currents and waves of life.

Orphic Mysteria

Orpheus, born of the Muse
Enchanter, charmer, wise one, Divine
Bard, Poet, and Prophet
drank many libations with Dionysus

This Mysteria lived each day
in constant communion
Through ritual and ceremony in dance
and transcendence

Ecstatic and cathartic release,
reflecting inner chambers of awareness
Expanding to commune and merge
with the Divine

Purifying the transient soul
with a joyous path through the Underworld
Each Initiates holding their golden passport
beyond death.

Sensing my question and curiosity, Kilo looked over.

"Why did these Mysteries decline?" I asked.

Klio continued, "These Mysteries dwindled due to various reasons. Some lost favor with the people and patrons. Over the centuries, the Mysteries evolved to align with changing cultures. Some traditions became distorted and controlled, while others diminished. In 380 CE, Emperor Theodosius I issued the edict of Thessalonica to close all the theaters and pagan temples as Christianity spread. What was not absorbed by the church was extinguished or hidden.

Recognizing this shift is crucial because humanity's inner landscapes have been molded and influenced for the past two millennia, if not longer. Some of these Mystery Initiates experienced an egoic death into rebirth. Those who once underwent the rituals shared a direct, intimate connection with the Divine without an intermediary. Many of these Mysteries were embedded with the Muse, guiding one to reach elevated states. We walked hand in hand with drums, songs, chants, dance, stories, and sacred words. These threads of inspiration awakened the senses and meditative states, altering consciousness and tethering to the Creative Spirit."

Klio glanced up at the waterfall.

"What today would allow one to immerse themselves fully in their power? What supports access to deeper levels of the psyche for release, purpose, and beyond the fear of death? This foundation of the Mysteries shows that all had access to certain wisdom, which allowed them to fully embrace life and death thousands of years ago. When the Pagan Gods and their rites fled underground, only one story of life, death, and resurrection remained. Access to the hidden Mysteries and their transformative power was reserved for a fortunate few. The rest of the population passed through an emissary."

Kilo closed the book, set it aside, and stood. "Alright, Initiate. Let us begin with a brief ritual to prepare you for your journey through Muse Mysteria. Please, rise."

"I've never performed a ritual."

"Most humans perform rituals daily. One's entire life is a ritual," Klio said as she deepened her breathing. She made a quick motion with her hand around the circle. White light emanated from the ring of water into a mist around us.

"Wait, how did you do that?" I asked. "Magic is real?"

"Of course. It's as real as your imagination. Everyone is doing magic each day. You just don't realize it—at some point, humanity will catch up. If you are comfortable, close your eyes and breathe deeply." Kilo said.

The white light whirled in the breeze. My body felt heavy, and pressure moved through my head. "What are we doing exactly?" I asked, flinching.

"We are removing a few blocks. There are beliefs and conditioning you've placed upon yourself that are interfering with your creativity. This will open you for the path ahead."

"We have to do this now? How long would it take me to do this on my own?"

"About six or seven years. Do you want to wait?" Klio asked.

"What! No, no, keep going." Determined not to waste years without a single page of writing. I haven't been able to write since my parents passed. Everything inside me felt stuck.

Klio moved closer, spinning her hand again. The pressure intensified. It was like being trapped in a wind tunnel. The sound emitted from deep within my body was deafening. A bitter taste filled my mouth, and my stomach tightened.

"You will be more at ease after this. Though there may be some discomfort from not living any other way."

"Sounds promising," I said, rubbing my side.

Klio twisted her wrist, and the pressure dissipated. Exhausted, I collapsed into my seat as the room spun.

"We can finish for the day. Someone will escort you to your room for the night, and a meal will be brought to you," she said

Chapter III
Entering the Muse Mysteries

"The soul, purified and reborn, rises again to the highest heavens."
—Dionysius of Halicarnassus

T HE MORNING SUN BATHED MY FACE. I waited for Klio at the central circle. My head throbbed, and my chest burned with rawness. It was my best sleep in years, with no midnight panic attacks. The table beside me was laid with hot tea and pastries. I poured a cup and selected a blueberry scone.

"Hello, Grace. I see you are awake. Are you ready to get started?" Kilo asked.

"Yes, as long as there are no wind tunnels today," I said.

She poured tea, stirred in a trace of honey, and tapped the cup with a spoon. "Sarcasm is welcomed here," she said, taking a sip.

"Let us dive into the Muse Mysteries," she said, revealing a purple book with gold-embossed symbols. It felt both timeless and new, enduring the ages yet remained untouched. She put on her reading glasses and began.

"To discover the Muse Mysteries, you must know that our temple never existed on the Earthly plane. However, sacred sanctuaries were established throughout Greece. Natural wells, springs, and rivers served as sacred sources of inspiration. Many seeking poiesis, 'poetry,' left offerings at such places to win our favor. East of Mount Helikon in the Valley of the Muses, a festival was held every four years. Many would gather to present dramas, songs, and music. A small theater was built with sculptures of each Muse surrounding the exterior. Some donated votive gifts to offer, honor, and petition us.

Another sanctuary rests where the rising sun in the east meets at the base of Mount Olympus: Leiberthra Sanctuary. This spot is home to Calliope's son Orpheus and was the original location for the Olympic games in music, poetry, and drama.

Priests in Delphi at the Temple made regular offerings to the Muses. Three of the Lyre's notes (low, middle, and high) were named accordingly as a Muse. The Priestesses may have played these notes as an induction for those who visited the Oracle."

At a particular moment in history, a shift took place. The Muse were tied to Mount Helikon and the Hippocrene Spring. This bridge to the land expounded and, with time, became conflated with Nymphs, Sirens, and eventually Faeries. Who were also downgraded from the Welsh word duw, which means Goddess or Divine."

Klio took off her glasses and held the book closer. "Are you listening?"

"Yes, I am surprised the original Olympic games included the arts, but what are the Muse Mysteries?"

"The source of the Muse Mysteries is a creative, energetic force and the play of life. We will go as deep as we can. The Mysteries are not easy to define. They reach out to you as a graceful activation of currents to experience, integrate, and live. It is coursing through each person, waiting to be unlocked. These patterns and energies encourage a person to find the key to remembrance and awakening. Initiating into the Muses' Mysteries is the *pathless path*, a mysterious journey further into oneness beyond the three directions or roads. The way through is inward.

The *pathless path* is one way of truth and liberation, where your true self is engaged with life as art and learns to live beyond outcomes, where creativity becomes a spiritual path. While outward rituals, practices, and performances exist, each Initiate finds their own path. In the Mysteries, an Initiate learns presence, flexibility, and comfort with uncertainty. You learn to develop and embrace your inner powers and form deeper relationships. The result is substantial growth.

This is what the ancient Mysteries did so well, guiding someone through life, death, and rebirth. After descending through death, the Muses stand at the threshold of life, helping the individual return to the world and to purpose. Engaging in life is part of the path and journey. One starts to live with true sight and intention in each moment. We guide you to create a foundation centered around your purpose and well-being. With the Muse and creative channels open, you learn to integrate and follow those threads that inspire and excite you. We move with you in co-creating a new story. Those new stories will change your inner tides. You will eventually witness a full emergence, and life will play differently within and around you. The *pathless path* might give the sense it is daunting and aimless, but contrary to this, it is a way to find the most incredible treasures."

The Rites of Rebirth

Klio set the book on the table. "Let's stretch our legs."

We set out for the trees past the eastern gate and ventured deeper into the forest to a grove. In the middle, an ancient stone circle surrounded by weathered ionic pillars reaching skyward. Below our feet, a mosaic intricately crafted into the shape of a nine-pointed star.

The theme of rebirth was prevalent in ancient Greece and reflected in their rites. Rebirth was a formal passage and the return to life with fresh eyes. The process belongs to the Divine Feminine, who is the catalyst for this awakening, but many have shifted from these energies. The usual reasons apply, such as fear of the unknown, safety, control, comfort, and security, but nothing develops in these conditions. In the modern world, your rites of passage have become more rooted in the material realm, emphasizing outer power and gain. But the outer powers don't provide you with an unshakable core because much of it is fleeting and conditional.

Many Gods, Goddesses, and Archetypes have experienced rebirths similar to those of humans. Remember, we are not stagnant; we evolve, shift, and transform. At times, we may lie dormant and are reborn when a specific pattern resurfaces. On the other side of this rite, one is granted an extraordinary inner power and no longer reliant on the outside world.

Your ancient ancestors told stories or performed rebirth rites. The most famous are the Eleusinian Mysteries, which tell of Persephone's emergence from the Underworld each spring. For six months, she symbolizes death and loss before leaving winter and entering the gate of renewal, honoring the cycle of rebirth each year.

There is the story of Dionysus, son of Zeus, and Semele, a mortal woman. In his youth, Dionysus was torn and ripped apart by the Titan Gods, which caused him to lose his sense of self and sanity. The Goddess Demeter finds him and restores his body, using her powers to regenerate him. He is reborn as a God with the power of Ecstasy.

The tale of the Phoenix from the Old Kingdom of Egypt tells the legend of a mythical bird that lived for thousands of years. The bird builds a nest for its death, then spontaneously bursts into flames. The Phoenix rises from its own ashes, born a mightier Being, and symbolizes the inevitability of destruction and the gift of death from the older self.

The well-known story of Osiris and Isis marks a complete transformation. In this recount, Osiris is dismembered by his brother and resurrected by the feminine force, his wife, Isis. Osiris is reborn with the power of two worlds, life and death.

In Norse mythology, Odin places himself upside-down on the World Tree, called Yggdrasil, for nine days and nights. A tree representing the Universal Womb resulted in him gathering the knowledge and wisdom of the Runes. His change in perspective, vulnerability, and self-sacrifice helped him transform into a God of great wisdom. The World Tree itself conducted the rite of his rebirth."

Klio unrolled her sleeves and pivoted to me.

"Initiate, I tell you these stories because they reveal that rebirth may cost us. But they will also bring forth greater wisdom, power, and gifts beyond what you perceive is possible.

Rebirth is a significant transformation in a person's life. This transition is spiritual and psychological. It can reflect a meaningful life change, such as moving through a dark night of the soul, undergoing significant healing, or transitioning into a new role. One may move through the birth canal at many points in one's life. Most of them are small shifts with fewer contractions.

Some will journey through a vast Void, emerging as a new Being, unrecognizable from the former self."

Klio stopped and brought her attention to one of the forest paths. We heard a ruffling of leaves. In the distance, the Wayfinder was navigating underbrush and pushing past branches.

"This way, Ella!" Klio waved.

Ella stumbled into the circle, brushing herself off and removing the sticks from her hair. "Huff," she said, setting her bag on the ground. She then took off her shoes and shook them out.

"Why did you take the western path? No matter. The Initiate is ready for the next part of the Mysteria," Klio said.

"I was feeling adventurous and seeking to go a different way. Perhaps I could have worn other shoes. We must head to the crossroads, which is this direction."

Chapter IV
The Torch and the Well

"It's not that things can't change, transform, or be dreamed into creation; it's a matter of whether you will surrender enough to let it happen." —J. Wells Kara

WE STOOD AT THE CROSSROADS. In front of us lay three winding paths stretching beyond sight. An eerie stillness lingered, with no breeze or birdsong to break the silence. Light diffused through the tree canopies. I could not tell if it was day or twilight.

"This is the one," said Ella.

Klio placed her belongings aside and opened a jar of gold pigment. She traced symbols onto Ella's palms.

"Initiate, hold out your hands," Klio invited. She painted sacred marks on my palms and continued her words. I felt my hands tingle with heat.

Kilo continued, "Before one initiates into the rite of rebirth, one must let go of the lingering past. This transition is especially for those in the Underworld who met the shadow and traveled too long through dark nights. I recognize you have traveled through these places. You have confronted many challenges and endured trials, gaining strength and resilience from such experiences. All of that has brought you to this moment. It is time to move on from the Underworld realm into the next phase of your journey. We will mark this transition at this crossroads. We will clear the way for you to go forward symbolically and energetically. These symbols will carry what is necessary for the path ahead and provide protection."

Ella unlatched her bulky bag and pulled out a wand. "Please stand back if you both will." She curled her hand around an elder branch and reached out her arm. Pointing to the North, she traced a door at the circle's edge. A power crept over me, and the hairs on my neck prickled. The wind began to howl, rising as if it, too, recognized the strange force she was evoking. Ella ascended both arms, and rays of light pierced around the threshold. A portal sprang open with a blaring sound, tearing through the middle realm.

We waited.

"Did you send the right signal?" Asked Klio, leaning over.

Ella leaned back, "Yes."

With force and flare, the portal crackled as a shadowy figure emerged. The Deity was cloaked in a black cloud. You could sense the ancient power they exuded. In another moment, the portal gleamed and closed, and the space around us fell into a deep silence.

Klio approached. "Welcome, Hekate, Queen of the Underworld."

Hekate held up her torch and squinted her eyes, "Muse, you have called?"

"Hekate, the Initiate who stands before you, has traversed through the Underworld of death. They are ready to enter into the promise of rebirth. As Muse, we seek to receive the torch, kindle their inner fire, and guide them in the middle realm of life."

Hekate lifted an eyebrow at Ella, "You could have called my name, but the elder branch is a nice touch."

Ella glanced at Klio and shrugged.

The Wise One casually waved a hand and twirled her cloak. Two large, imposing black wolves with piercing amber eyes appeared and raised their heads. "Muse, these two will determine if the Initiate is ready."

With intention, the giant wolves quietly circled me, twitching their noses, sniffing and smelling for fear, shadows, and confusion inside me. Standing still, trying not to pet the majestic creatures, I debated if my journey through the darkness and wind tunnel had dispelled and released enough. It's challenging to know when one is ready.

I saw a hint of amusement in Hekate's eyes as she watched me closely. Satisfied, the hounds swiftly sat and leaned against Hekate's side. She patted their heads and threw two savory raw bones to the ground. Hekate made her way to me with her torch. "Muse, you may take the flame of this torch and close this one's Underworld work for now."

"As for you, Grace, the wisdom of the sacred dark will guide you the same way as the Celestials. Even though you will perform this transition, I will watch from afar. As you traverse the middle realm, know it is the most challenging. With the Muse as your guide, you will learn to bring your true self, gifts, and purpose to the world."

She abruptly veered. "Raise the torch, Muse, as I pass this flame to you."

Klio ceremonially brought over her sacred torch and held it out with both hands. Hekate spoke a blessing as she extended and ignited the flame. Sparks flared, transmuting purple and blue into a mixture of an iridescent fire. The Crone stepped closer, "Be sure to take care of this Initiate, Muse." She raised her hand, and with a snap of her fingers, the portal reopened. The wolves kicked their hind legs and leaped through. As she crept toward the veil, she glimpsed back at me, winked, and passed through.

"Ah, I think that went well." Ella cheered.

Spark of the Inner Well

We made our way back to the stone circle. With the flaming torch, Klio gestured for me to join her at the center. "The Muse possesses both fire and water, hand in hand. As you will learn, these opposite elements work together in the creative process. With this ceremony, you will pass from the lessons of the sacred dark to rebirth and integrate into the world as a creator."

"This flame lights your path and reveals your inner well of creation." Klio held the torch between us. A golden hue illuminated her as she chanted a sacred incantation. With a gentle breath, she blew the flame into me. The power and magic of the Divine fire passed over my skin, through my body, and into the depths of me. The essence of this flame's ancient activation spread and surged through me.

Ella softly spoke, "Prepare yourself to visit the Well of Creation and cross the threshold of rebirth. Allow yourself to receive these energies as they move into your life. This process is between you, the Muse, and the Divine. You are answering and acknowledging the call from your creative self. Many things will continue to fall away as you walk further into your authentic self. Lay down the sword and pick up the cup. In time, these waters will pour over your imagination, your inner landscape, and back into the world. This is not a fast process but a slowing down. You must discern whether this is right for you at this juncture. If you feel called to go deeper into growth and change. The Muse will take you further into their Mysteries. You will journey into the realm of imagination, creativity, and intuition to empower them to unfold. When you are ready, move to the center.

"I accept the call. I am ready," I said, acknowledging the intention.

Klio walked north, lit the other torches around the circle's perimeter, and lowered her hood. She pressed her hands together and expanded the space's energy field.

Ella continued. "Gaze at the center of this circle." The central stone trembled and faded, revealing a natural well brimming underneath. "Reach into your inner well of creation, Initiate. Allow its energetic stream to flow into you. Surrender to its lifeforce. It gives you power and inspiration. All Beings have this creative reserve in them, a magical well." Ella's voice intensified. "Do you remember this part of yourself? Step inward and immerse yourself. Let it replenish and wash away the burdens and barriers. Allow the water to purify every aspect of you. Remember all that has held you back from your creative self. Speak them out loud into the well for release. With each word Initiate, see them dissolving and transforming. I will witness."

I lowered to my knees and cast out my words.

"Well, of creation, I release this deep depression that fills my body and mind, stealing the very essence of life. Its shadow has consumed me for too long.

Well of creation, I speak and surrender the struggle, the emptiness, and the loss of my parents. I release the vast and unrelenting grief, heartache, and mourning.

Well of creation, I let go of disappointments and rejections and all of those who dimmed my expression and light. Who didn't believe in me, care, or love me.

Dissolve and transform all the ways I self-sabotage, hide, ignore, and avoid my spirit and gifts!"

Ella sat beside me. "Are you ready to call in everything you need and desire and set your intention?"

"Yes," I said, exhausted.

Klio whispered and summoned more light, intensifying and protecting the space around us. Ella maneuvered to the opposite side of the sacred waters and poised the elder branch. She twirled her hand over the well with a flourish, transforming the spoken words. The water swished and swirled.

Ella lifted her hands and voice. "It is time to invoke and speak your intention for the path ahead. What is it you need and desire on your journey?"

I stood, placed a hand on my heart, closed my eyes, and waited for the words to come. Until now, no one had ever asked me what I truly needed. I had always struggled to stand in my power and voice my desires. A tightness formed in my throat. Feeling the weight of this moment, my hand instinctively went to my neck, and my voice broke free.

"I call forth my creative self for the path ahead. I invite the Divine spark to fully merge with my life. I call on my courage. I summon my strength. I surrender to Divine wisdom and offer my light to the world. I desire a sovereign life of inner wisdom, filled with love, creativity, abundance, and joy."

Klio whispered and calmed the energy.

Ella lowered her hands onto the stone circle. Gold and white light streamed from the ground and pillars, surrounding us in a sphere of protection. "Initiate, you are ready to meet the Muses and their stories."

PART II

Muse Self-Initiation

Chapter V
Klio: Muse of the Past & Wisdom

"We start with history, we reflect, then we purge." —Priestess

ELLA BRUSHED HER HANDS TOGETHER, SHOOK THEM OUT, AND CROSSED TO THE OUTER CIRCLE. "The circle of protection is cast. All in a day's work."

Klio glared sideways at Ella, "Finished?"
"Oh, yes, yes—finished."
The Muse proceeded to the other side of the well, across from me. I eagerly sat, not sure what was to come.

Klio, The Proclaimer, lifted her hand and trumpet.
"A call to the past, a call to the present. Where sound waves meet water beyond the river's mouth and flow over ancient stones. Every movement, wrinkle, scar, and uttered word you use comes from an embedded past of your making or inheritance. Memories are etched from what one learns. I am the movement of memory in time.

When the tides and cycles shift, let them move through you. Resistance to change will only lead to turbulent waves or stagnant waters. For the wise are those who learn that the past and future are the same.

Don't let the past grip you too tightly, nor hold you too close to your identity. Instead, wear it like a long, flowing robe."

Kilo's Scroll

Klio sat beside me.

"Grace, let me tell you my story, what came before."

Part I – What Realms May Come

Long ago, in the midst of childhood, I found a place beyond the realm of my knowledge. In wild fields and summer's grace, I found myself running past hollyhocks, irises, and time. Even in haste, I did not disturb them. They were living their purpose.

The sky reached out to me that day as I ran past the flowers and trees. Through a veil of flashing light, a thick echo pierced my ears and sight. I landed in a library, with halls stretching as far as one could see and towering books over me. The library summoned me that day to show my fate and what's to be.

I ran my fingers over the titles and sleeves when something caught my eye. In the middle of the hall, on the floor, was a brown book with vibrant, striking pages. I picked it up with both hands and read aloud *Klio: Muse of the Past & Wisdom*. As I flipped through the pages, several chapters were blank.

"This is your fate," Mother said. Her hands are on her hips, and her head to the right. She bent over and scooped me up tight. "How did you ever find your way, my precocious one? You were supposed to wait a few more years." She laughed.

"This book says my name, but the pages are blank?"

"There are books that have yet to be written. Once an event occurs in one's life, their story appears. Other books are written eons prior to one's birth. The library is mysterious and operates from its own will. When you are ready, honey, these halls will tell you of its wisdom."

"Mom, did you create this place?"

"You could say I had a hand in some of it, but it's way older than me."

Mneme was, and still is, a loving and generous mother, full of curiosity, though sometimes easily distracted. After offering a brief explanation, she left me with the books and wandered off to read the latest entries. What caught her attention, I can't quite say. In my formative years, I spent hours hidden away. Studying while my sisters were dancing and singing with play. I enjoyed the solitude and quiet but wondered if Mother left the library to keep an eye on me? As Mother's apprentice, she told stories and myths. How it shaped all things. She excelled at storytelling, while I preferred researching, playing music, and pondering how the past shaped us.

Let me not get ahead of myself. Mneme drifted off during a session, leaving me with a mountain of work. Feeling annoyed, I opened a book called *The Alchemy of Past Imprints*. Scanning through the information piqued my interest. It reads: *"In the Middle Realm, fusing the Elements with a human's past imprints initiates a sacred transmutation. This is an alchemical fire known as calcination."* Can this happen to us? I continue reading. *"Gods and Goddesses are not flameproof. Calcination burns off the tendencies even in immortals."* Why hasn't anyone spoken about this? I bookmarked it and set it aside to dive into later.

I advanced to the second book, *The Source From Which All Things Appear*. I blew the dust off the cover and coughed. *Who cleans this place?* Unsealing the cover, I flipped to a painted page written in a distant language. I ran my fingers over the raised paper and studied the words until I heard someone calling me.

"Kleos, Kllleeoos."

Not entirely my name, though it clearly drew my attention. At first, I thought it was Mneme. I wandered through the book section, searching for her. Stopping, I lowered my glasses at a strange orb. A blue bubble of light flew at me. *How out of place? Definitely not mother,* I thought. The bookshelves rattled, and the floor clattered as the orb transformed into a woman so radiant I could barely make out her outline. The Manifestation approached.

"Muse and Keeper, be unafraid; I am here as a Guide and have called. You are meeting your destiny, as you did eons ago. I offer this scroll of the past and of time. When you behold any Being, you will sense their making and what will be written. You are to guide and ensure humanity remembers, learns, and releases.

"Bright Goddess, what do you mean eons ago?" The scroll dropped and bounced across the floor to me. She was gone.

"Hello?"

I reached for the scroll. A shock and jolt of energy blasted through my body. I arched in pain as my mind opened like a funnel. Visions poured in, revealing the wisdom of creativity and transmuting old wounds. I saw humans weaving countless webs, creating illusions that tore through the collective. Their stories shape the generations to come. As the vibrations and visions intensified, I expanded further. Seeing one affects all. My awareness settled back into the room.

My body trembled as the fire continued to cascade through me. I lay the scroll on the table, filled a glass with water, drank, and stared at the rolled-up papyrus. "Kopros."

Part II – The Fate of Things

During warm summer nights, the family would sit on the veranda surrounded by fireflies, cypress trees, and olive groves. The Fates would tell us stories
about the universe and what was to come. They imparted the plans of the
Gods and mortals in prophecies and possibilities. The Moirai, or the Fates
as you call them today, are a mysterious trio said to have been born from the
oldest primordial, Nyx, at the inception of the universe. The youngest, Clotho,
spins the thread of birth. Lachesis determines the length of the thread of one's
life. And the most ancient one, Atropos, cuts the thread at death. They dwell
beyond time and space, watching over the cosmos, and are regarded by the
most powerful Gods and Goddesses.

I was a child when Atropos became our Godparent, prompted by Zeus leaving Mother with nine children. They explained some events were inevitable,
while others lived with flexibility and choice. The Fates were constantly at the
house sewing stories into each of us for safekeeping.

One evening, I slipped away from their gathering to the northern spring
and sat under one of the oaks heavy with acorns. Rolling a few in my hand,
I threw them one by one, aiming for the center of the water.

"Careful, the spring might throw back, or worse!"

"Atropos! I was seeking to sit with the quiet trees."

"Quiet? Do you know how old this oak is? Kilo, does this have to do with a
certain papyrus sitting in a library?"

My eyes shifted to the side. "I was going to ask how you knew, but how
would you not know?"

"Kilo, you are going to figure out its mystery. It is easier if you don't resist
your gifts. Bundled gifts weigh down the mind; I'd much prefer it if you didn't
implode under the pressure.

"I have not told Mneme."

"The scroll is not her destiny; she would be happy if that is your concern.
Do you know how much she loves her daughters?"

Atropos hugged me close. "The answers will come, Kilo. They are inside you. Allow them to bloom. Come. Stop bothering the living waters. Let's see what Mneme has in the kitchen."

Part III – A Woven Thread

The morning sun drifted through the south window, its rays touching the scroll. I directed my attention to the book titles on the shelves and paced. *Why am I afraid?*

Removing all the books from the desk. I placed the papyrus in the middle and pulled the string free. Relieved by no shock, I gently unrolled the thick, smooth paper. Images, words, and symbols rippled over the surface, whispering. They were moving, breathing, and alive. It stirred perspective within me. Impressions of all things past flooded my mind. Significant events, astonishing deeds, and accomplishments were etched into myths, symbols, and legends. These stories were reminders that the future reflected the past. The scroll revealed that every Being lives the myth of its making and what it needs to learn or change.

Many mortals are called to a tale beginning far away in an unknown land, searching for life's meaning and redemption. A quest through the valleys of fear, love, and desires. Unclaimed territory reflects itself on the world stage. Some have yet to discover this place. A land with many hidden valleys, guardians, dense forests, and buried treasures.

As the words mingled, I saw patterns repeating for thousands of years within individuals and the collective. These landscapes have shaped humanity and continue to impact the fabric of life. Connections persisting for eons, resonating with the power of a spell. Some stories are beneficial. Other stories linger in the mind for years and may even reveal themselves as injuries or ailments in the body. The scroll also warned about determinants not to incite in oneself or fellow philos, 'friends.'

Names of storytellers hovered over the paper, the keepers of the culture. They held the keys to the past and molded the future. They embodied myths from the stars, the land, and each season. They sang their chants to the ground and spoke to the stones. Their names still wander in Gaea and live on the pages of time.

History is alive and carries power. It's not up to Muse to determine how the energy is wielded. I recognized my purpose as a catalyst, a notion, an inspiration. When a story from the past dissolves, it resolves itself for the future.

The scroll showed me that creativity and purpose live within all. It is more about removing the conditioned layers that have caused one to search the world to mirror back the self. One of the differences between Gods, Goddesses, and mortals is that we live and are the full expression of our essence.

It was getting late. I flipped the scroll over to straighten and close it. As my hand shifted over the paper, I was startled as the ink morphed into lines. Faint images emerged, forming an ancient floor plan with a circle at its center. It was the library! The dimensions went way beyond the physical aspect of the building into areas yet explored. I had to find out its mysteries.

I gently rolled up the scroll, tied it three times, and placed it under one of the floorboards.

Journey to the Key of the Creative Self

"If you will settle in, I will guide you on a journey to your inner landscape,"
Klio said, sitting and taking a few deep breaths. Ella took out a small drum
and began a light, deepening rhythm.

Please get into a comfortable position. This journey will lead you to find the key to your creative self. Notice your body and breathe deeply in and out a few times. Look toward your eyebrows and keep breathing. Gently close your eyelids. Allow the breath to slow down as your body sinks further into the seat or floor. Relax even more. "Bring your attention to your feet. Imagine the soft green grass beneath them; feel it beneath your toes. Go deeper into the experience. (Pause)

Begin to see colors and shades shifting around you. Listen to the sounds that surround you. Turn toward the center of the stone circle and sacred well, where a Priestess of the Past greets you. Follow her to a threshold and a doorway. Notice everything around you. (Pause)

This is the passage to find the key; it will take you to your creative self. Whatever you encounter has influenced you in this life. It does not need to make sense. The information you gain is what you need to know. You must find the key and ask it to lead you to your creative self. The Priestess opens the door and will wait for you. (Pause)

Begin to make your way back from this journey. Bring the key you have found, your creative self, and what you have discovered. Make your way back to the stone circle and sacred well. Leave an offering for the Priestess. (Pause)

Slowly return to where you started on this journey, the green grass and the room.

Klio's Well-Wish

"Initiate, I have brought you this far through the Muse Mysteria. Time for you to venture to the next Muse, Melpomene. You may journey to my realm and your creative self at any time. Ella will guide you through the Hall. Before you go, I leave you with a gift. Remember, time is a movement, and it is also an illusion. You have not been born, nor will you pass. Your Being, your vessel, searches to fulfill its desires and live its story. I offer you these good wishes on your journey. Sit and open to these words and blessings I share with you."

It's time to
ease your mind, Seeker
lay down the reflections
of the daunting past.

It's time to
put down those tasks
forgive, close doors
and move on.

It's time to
open to the unknown
to shine your light
on wounds and lost places.

It's time to
allow yourself
freedom and pleasure
to taste the senses.

It's time to
make way for the
creative self and soul
To enliven your life and path once more...

My love and many blessings,
Klio

Chapter VI
Melpomene: Muse of Tragedy

"In the end, we are all just stories." —*Heraclitus*

ELLA GUIDED ME BEYOND THE STONE CIRCLE, THROUGH A CLEARING, AND BACK INTO THE HALL. I had a queasy stomach; it was hard to say goodbye to Klio, who had guided me this far on the journey.

"We will take the next right," said Ella.

At the end of the corridor, I noticed the walls moving. "What is happening?"

"Quite normal. You transformed a part of yourself, so the Hall will shift according to your path." She stated.

The Hall diverted left to a winding walkway. We passed archaic, weathered, and modern doors. Ella paused in front of a black-paneled entryway with a worn brass handle. Her eyes narrowed, and her mouth twitched to the side with uncertainty.

"Shouldn't you know if it's the right door?"

Ella cleared her throat. "I am ensuring you are ready to proceed to the Muse of Tragedy."

"Ready? How deep are we going?"

"Let me say, deep enough to need a strong cup of tea and a good cry afterward. Oh, and you might question your entire life."

"You can't be serious!"

"Let me listen," she said, closing her eyes. "Yes, this is the one. Again, knock and enter, I'll be waiting for you."

I knocked and hesitated for a moment, then turned the handle. A wave of tension flooded my chest as the entrance creaked open. My throat tightened, and my breath was rapid. *Okay, let's do this.*

Inside, Nightingales sang a soulful melody while the stars spun and bloomed above me. It was a balmy night filled with shadows of ancient pines and poplars. Silhouettes of the trees swayed in slow, hypnotic movements. The breeze was thick with the scents of moss and myrtle. The sensual darkness wrapped around me, and my senses expanded. A glowing light approached the trees. I crouched behind the foliage.

"Behold! Initiate, show yourself. Rise and meet me," the Muse called out.

I nearly jumped out of my skin. Mustering my courage, I made my way to the clearing. Melpomene gazed at me through a black and gold mask.

"Stand before me, Initiate. You who have traversed my realm many times. You who have plunged into the deepest of waters. You who have tried to steer the ship of emotions to escape surrendering. Unbeknownst to you was the life vest of Muse. Your sadness is a song many don't hear and a place many fear. A story of loss, of grief, of despair and you are here."

I felt the familiar grief welling up inside. Agitated and angry, I snapped.

"Why have I never returned from your depths?! Why have I drifted through a haze of endless days, isolated and suffocating under sorrow? Too fatigued to create, I live in an invisible battle, swinging a blunt sword, constantly hacking at despair."

"You have come to find out why tragedy is a Muse. You hope to find the secret key to ending your suffering. Am I right?

Grace, you have befriended your tears. You have grown attached to your mourning and become blind to the lessons. You've forgotten that vulnerability and surrender open you to the awakening of life once again. Hold this paradox. I am the movement of chaos and liberation and reside in the innermost chamber of the heart. One way to reach me is through the deepest, darkest doldrums of sorrow; this is one path of life and love. Grief is the most misunderstood emotion in the entire pantheon of feelings. At some point, one will encounter me. The price may be heartbreak, yet it initiates one into the greater Mysteries of Love."

Grief is a heavy, long cloak that descends without warning. It is unrelenting and lives on its own terms. Most will attempt to avoid the waters of heartache, despair, and disappointment. Going against currents and paddling over emotional waves takes strength. Yet, these wounds create an opening that can be filled with the gold of forgiveness, acceptance, and love.

As Muse, I move through you to decompose roles, beliefs, limitations, and things that never came to be. You have outgrown them. If you deny your grief, it will seep into the corners of your life. It may affect you in ways you may not recognize.

I am your companion in this realm and can show you the way through. The valley of tragedy is bumpy; it travels along hidden streams, under heavy stones, and in the shadows of forgotten canyons. I will show you how to mourn well, celebrate life, and bury the previous self behind.

In the end, liberation."

Holding Tragedies Mask

Allow me to tell you how I became the Muse of Tragedy. Like Klio and the other Muses, I once loved a mortal. A love that is neither unheard of nor forbidden among the Gods. We seldom speak of these relationships, as such passions are fleeting. They are owned by time and leave us scars that rarely heal.

Part I – The Radiant Dreamer

Many years before the great flood, a farmer lived at the edge of Anatolia with seven brothers, all hardworking and exceptional in their own way. Hartasili, a gifted dreamer, stood out to me. He was a radiant man with a bright, burning heart and eyes lit with a curious nature. I can still see him walking on the barley hill planted by him and his family. He was tall with curly, dark, floppy hair, a broad, inviting smile, and soft blue eyes.

He saw me wandering past his land and waved with confidence. "Hello! Hey!" He ran over to catch up with me. Breathing heavily, he asked, "Are you lost?" His concern of my journeying through this wild, remote, and lush area was not unwarranted. I risked these long ventures alone. And why I called to the Fates as protectors.

"I'm heading to the northern lands."

"That is far from this hill and several sunsets." He glanced to the sky, "Night's near. Come join my family for bread and wine."

Sensing no threat, I agreed. "Yes, thank you." How can a Muse say no to such a sweet invitation?

There was a reason this man called upon the Muse. I found myself compelled to stay on his farm with his loving family. Our paths had woven us together for a purpose I had yet to comprehend.

As the weeks passed, I stared out the window to catch glimpses of him in the fields. I watched the sweat beading over his brow. Early some mornings, he was in the kitchen covered in flour, making flatbread for the coming days. I watched his bouts of laughter with his family in the evenings as I sat nearby, sipping and clutching my cup of wine. "Late at night, I found him sketching by candlelight, using small sticks of charcoal. I had grown infatuated."

A morning later, he tapped on my door. "Melli, would you like to go for a ride?"

I touched the door. A smile flashed over me. "Yes."

The morning was cool. I wrapped a top layer around my waist, secured it with a cloth, and left the house. Hartasili waved me over to the fence. Two stocky horses with long manes were waiting.

"Have you ridden before Melli?"

"Once, a while ago, but he was too wild and didn't listen."

"I have been working with these two for some time now, and they are wild, but with all the food and shelter we provide them, they have become accustomed to us. The black one is Tas, and the one with the white spots is Nisa."

He patted and stroked their necks and placed several layers of thick brown and green fabric over their backs.

I stood next to Nisa and brushed her white feather-like mane. Her doe eyes were calm and sensitive.

"She likes you, which will make the trip much easier."

"Trip?"

"Yes, over the hill, not far. There is a curious place I found. Are you ready?" He knelt to the ground. "Place your foot in my hands, and I'll lift you over."

I braced my hand on his shoulder and felt his warm muscles contracting.

"Melli, jump and swing your leg over when I say go. Yes?"

I nodded, mesmerized by his full lips glistening in the sunlight.

"Go!"

I hopped onto Nisa and attempted to swing my leg over, but I landed flat on my stomach across her back. My arms were outstretched, and my lungs were gasping for air.

"Hang on, try to slide your leg over, and grab the mane. The mane, Melli!"

Startled, Nisa backed into the fence, launching herself into a straight buck. I tried to grab her long mane but was thrown sideways, heading toward the ground. In anticipation, Hartasili dove forward and caught me. Nisa bolted, tearing across the field and into the trees.

We were both stunned, staring at each other in disbelief. In my narrow survival, I burst out laughing. Hartasili exhaled in relief as he dusted off my robe.

"Are you okay?"

"Yes, fine. What are we going to do?"

"Tas will take us."

Unfazed, Tas lowered his head and leisurely chewed on a clover patch. Hartasili gently patted his neck, stepped back, and made a flawless leap, landing in one smooth motion.

"Tas trusts you, doesn't he?"

"Give me your hand, I'll pull you up."

I reached for him and jumped, narrowly making it over.

"Hold onto me tight."

I pulled his sturdy body close and rested my head on his back. He smelled of a mixture of juniper and earth. His scent was so inviting that I pressed my nose into his clothing. This man was a home I had never had, a dream I had long desired.

Over the hill, the valley dipped into a dense forest. Several trails veered to the left and right, but one trail—a person might overlook lay straight ahead. Tas entered as if he knew which way to go, trotting high over the grasses and field flowers. The path grew thicker with foliage as we passed through a veil into another world. I felt a subtle shift around me. The trail gradually widened into a clearing. Tas stopped, lowering his head to munch on the grass. Hartasili slid to one side and hopped to the ground."

"I will catch you, don't worry."

Trusting him, I fell into his arms. Tingles shook throughout my body. My cheeks flushed.

"Let me show you what I discovered; it's not far ahead. Shut your eyes." He took my hand to guide me, parting the thick reeds as we stepped over stones and uneven ground. I listened to the sweeping grass until I felt him stop.

"Okay, Melli."

As I opened my eyes, I gasped. The elated beauty struck me. A waterfall poured into smaller pools and plunged into a vibrant turquoise-blue spring surrounded by wispy trees. Hartasali cupped the water and brought it to his mouth. "It's pure."

I lowered and touched the surface; the sunlight amplified its nature, but the current and sound caught my interest. I sensed a backdrop of influence. I dipped my hand into the cool water and centered myself. Rubbing my fingers together, the pool felt like the finest linen. Prickles ran over my shoulders and neck, and I heard a faint underlay of chatter. A euphoric sensation arose when I dabbed the water on my lips."

"How did you discover the spring?"

"Many years ago, Tas and I were on one of the trails, and I heard a woman singing. Tas heard her, too; his ears perked. We went off the trail and found this spot, but this site was empty. The singing was different. It called me."

"I believe you happened upon an enchanted spring. Does anyone else know about this?"

"No one."

This was magic, but not one of the Muse. Who could the enchanter be?

"Melli, are you okay?"

"Oh, yes, it's the most incredible thing I have seen in a long time. Perhaps we can come back another day?" I took his hand, guiding us back to Tas. He pulled back.

"Are you sure you want to leave?"

"Yes, let's come another day. Can you lift me up on Tas again?"

He took the south trail around into the valley. I noticed a willow tree with a canopy of silver-green leaves sweeping like brushstrokes. Its gray trunk reached far into the sky, and its branches wide. A subtle brook flowed by its roots.

"Squeezing him to me, I gestured. "What of that tree?"

"It has been in this valley forever. Our ancestors consider it born of these lands."

"Can I have a closer look?"

He pressed Tas with his heel in its direction.

Stopping, I carefully slid and jumped down.

"Are you hungry? I brought some bread and wine." He asked.

I gave a nod and stood by the tree. A subtle frequency sprang from its roots into the trunk and sky. The soft breeze through the branches mesmerized me. There was a charm to this place, a power between worlds. Colors became more vivid, subtle sounds louder, and the water smoother. I helped Hartasili lay out the food on the woven blanket. As we sat, time slowed to a dream.

Part II – A Union Between the Worlds

Sitting beneath the majestic tree
him beside me in a dream yet to be
A forgotten song from ages past
stirred within him, glowing at last
The branches swayed incantations
my senses shifted to each sensation

Our hunger rose as we settled in
spinning pleasures beneath our skin
Flatbreads, honey, and delicious treats
licking his fingers dripping with sweets
The fullness of wine on my tongue
its velvety warmth, a song unsung

His parted lips, close to mine
enchanting, ever-pure, and Divine
Our kisses echoed, deep connection
a vivid dance and sweet reflection

A force and magic transcendence
beyond the timeless, ascended

Gently, he laid me softly down
loosened my clothes and blue gown
My hands through his thick, dark hair
pulling him closer, drawing him near
Lifting his tunic, he revealed to me
a sculpted bronze God, steady and free

He pressed his sultry skin onto mine
as I watched his beauty shine
Our passion sparked, a flame quickened
his motions deepened, feelings thickened
A warmth filled us, making us whole
Coming together, our connection of soul

My heart, with waves of ecstasy
Pure bliss undulating inside me
Entwined in the cradle of his arms,
Held captive by his endless charms
I surrendered and found release
the world around us faded and ceased.

What mystery did he have on me?
What love, may this be?

Part III – The Hill of Tragedy

We returned to the house as evening fell. By late night, the winds howled, and the house groaned. Side by side, we lay. The amber fire crackled, and the brook outside murmured. He ran his fingers through my fine hair.

"Melli, have you no union with another man?"
"If you are asking if I have bonded with someone, no. Why?"
"Because of your beauty and strength. And your ability to ride wild horses."
We laughed.

"You're sweet. My family comes first, and my travels are distant.

Hartasili slid closer and propped his head. "Will you join me? You can bring your family to my land."

Holding my breath, I watched the fire and gave him no answer. His eyes shifted to the ceiling, searching for the words. I had to check with the Fates. At least, that is what I told myself to avoid the conversation. Muses can bond to a mortal, but we must speak of our origins. In the past, humans have not taken this news well. Though, he may have sensed my otherworldliness. He said I was a magic he could not name a few days ago. And there was a different aura about him that I couldn't place. I reached across his chest and held him.

"Did you hear the willow tree earlier today? I heard its song in the distance."

He sat up. "You heard it? I thought I was the only one!"

Fall was shifting, and the cold was nearing. Frost started to sprinkle the fields. A thin layer of icy snow was on the hills. We walked hand in hand, trudging through the slush and mud as our breath met the crisp wind. He stopped, shifted his feet, and brushed the side of his hair. He took my hand and pressed it to his chest. "Will you bond with me in the Spring after seeds meet soil?" I felt an urge and impulse to tell him and could hold back no longer.

My lips quivered as I caressed his brow and cheek. I so favored him. I began to speak of my birth, the past, and how we would not age the same way. Our relationship would never resemble that of a bonded family, for one cannot cling tightly to a Muse. As I continued, he grew heavy with each word. He let go of my hand and staggered back, covering his eyes in disbelief and with an anguished cry. "Ohhhh, I knew you were different! By the Gods!" For a moment, he stood, laboriously breathing, speechless, bent forward in pain, gripping his heart as if a sword had mortally wounded him. He gasped for breath. My chest tightened; sensing his pain, I reached for him. He fell forward and took hold of my hand. Our love locked eyes as he collapsed lifeless.

Hartasaili. Hartasili!

He did not move.

"Wake up!"

A roar of thunderous fear and pain ripped through me. I felt the sharp claws of grief grip and clench me.

"AaaAHHHHHH!" I cried to the greater Gods, but only clouds gathered, and hard rain descended.

Along the outer ridge, my sisters stood beside the Goddess of Death. "NO! You can't take him. No, NOT YET!"

In the evening, Polyhymnia raised her arms and sang a gentle hymn for his crossing. The Goddess touched my shoulder. I held Hartasili's arm and brushed his cold skin as I purified him before draping white linen over his body. I paused, longing for his eyes to open.

My sisters lowered their heads. The saddened brothers removed their hats.

I mourned for a thousand years, the tears endless.

Part IV – Gift from the Underworld

A guiding hand tugged me back from the darkness and isolation.

"It's time to join the world again," Kilo said.

I collapsed in anguish. "I am unsure if enough time has passed, Kilo. The grief only reminds me of him. I am torn. My Being empty and far from shore, the waves of pain ceaseless and relentless. What have I done?"

"My sister, grief flows as shifting tides; even the wisest can not predict its nature."

Reluctantly, I reentered life to help Kilo with the library. My days were filled with dusting stacks of weathered books and herding the missing ones to their proper shelves.

"Didn't you return 'Time in Reverse' to the shelf yesterday?"

"Yes, in the natural physics section, like you asked."

"Hmm, let's take a break and meet later. I have to figure out what the library is trying to tell me." Kilo said.

I walked into the garden for an overdue rest when a subtle presence stirred the stillness. Beyond the fountain, a dark-robed Goddess appeared from a cool, wet mist. A tremendous luminous light sparkled around her dark features. Her feet, barely touching the ground, were covered with soot. Her keys chimed and rang. The scent of ancient bones covered the bright roses, Queen of the Underworld. Hekate, I know her well.

"Melpomene, you have sunk so far into the waters of grief you have stepped into my realm. You are welcome, but this is not your fate. Muse, I come with an offering for your wound."

"Have you come with Hartasili? Is he here?!"

"Dear Muse, Hmph. We have rules about mortal death. Hartasili is in my world, the unseen. You will recall that each God, Goddess, and Muse have their own domain."

The Goddess unveiled a dark, ornate box with etchings. With a fluid motion, her long fingers unlocked the clasp, revealing its mysterious contents.

"This will show you how to work with tragedy. You, my dear, are its keeper. This will be your gift to the mortals. You will bring those withered with wounded hearts back to the living and present. Many don't belong in my realm—yet. For this Muse, you will have three days a year when the veils thin to visit Hartasili. The Fates have already spoken their prophecies. He will return to the middle world of form."

"Only three days!"

"Child, it's what I can offer without causing much unrest!" She grasped the magical keys as if to keep them from listening.

Lifting the black and gold beaded mask, I sensed its power. It poured through my arms into the inner chambers of my heart. A piercing tug pulsated over my chest. A powerful force surged into the broken, empty spaces. I pressed my hand to my chest, clenching my teeth. My eyes burned as tears spilled forth in release. Sobbing, I felt hope, joy, and love rising within me, pulling me back to life.

"Why are you doing this, Hekate!"

"Do you want the answer?"

"Yes, don't cross me!"

"Dearest, most don't want to hear or accept these words. Sigh. A call within you drew you to your gifts. The tragedy left you vulnerable and became the gateway to your hidden strength. As your heart shattered, its capacity for love forged a deeper connection. It grew, opening you beyond what you could imagine with the Divine Source. The mask you bear is the key that will spark the light, awakening the heart's return to the living, Melpomene. In time, you will come to sense its beauty."

The Crone wrinkled a smile. See you when the veil's thin, my Muse." And with a whirl, she vanished.

The Mourners

Invoked with song and sadness
the veiled ones held the center, the gate of transition
—bridges to the afterlife

They stood at the portal
guiding the dead to the other side
—beyond all who mourn

The soul's journey
beyond flesh and time, a rite of passage
—toward the arms of the Divine

Living in bereavement
moving through grief, feeling the opened cracks
—of the wounded heart

The Mourners
carrying tragedy's mask, engaged with its spirit
—dancing us back at last

Journey with Tragedies Mask

Melponmene sits down next to you. *"Initiate this journey is an opportunity to view grief through the mask's lens. I am presenting this journey to help you process and release. Grief often takes a lot of space and vitality in the inner and outer world. This can hinder creativity, stifle connections, and block the flow of life. You will meet a Priestess of the Underworld who works alongside me and is experienced in the process."*

Find a place to relax. Notice your body and its boundaries from the top of your head to the tip of your toes. Expand fully into the body and sink into the seat, cushion, or floor. Bring your attention to your breath. Take a deep breath in. Exhale slowly through the mouth. Continue at your own pace. As you inhale again, gently lift your eyes toward your eyebrows. As you exhale, close your eyes. Allow your body to relax and deepen with each breath, sinking down further and further into a state of calm.

Sense the presence of a beautiful forest on a bright, sunny day. Feel the breeze, inhale the scented fragrance of the flowers. Notice each tree around you. Breathe the fresh air. You are safe. As you venture deeper into the forest, you notice a Priestess on another trail walking toward you. She greets you and leads you through the forest to a stone circle.

Within the circle, she pulls a mask from beneath her cloak. This mask carries all the stories and experiences of tragedy and sadness in your life. Notice its features, colors, and design. When you put on the mask, you will witness a different world and discover parts of yourself that have yet to grieve or things you are still carrying. When you wear the mask, a hidden landscape or event will emerge. Whatever comes up, allow the story to unfold; it may not make sense initially, but go with whatever surfaces.

The Priestess holds the mask out to you, and you take it into your hands. Remember to hold the creative key you have found; it will guide you and keep you safe. When you're ready, put on the mask. Take note of the landscape, story, or event unfolding. Ask the key to reveal the story or pattern limiting your creative self. Take your time. (Pause)

In a moment, you will return to the stone circle. Take in any remaining details. (Pause)

When you are ready, remove the mask. The Priestess stands in front of you, wearing her mask and holding a staff. Her large, dark eyes peer deep into you. In her eyes, it reflects the pain you have hidden. The Priestess recognizes what you have tucked away, avoided, or adapted into anger. Nurturing, she is compassionate about why you have held these things so close for so long. The Priestess points the staff to a river not far from the stone circle. This is the river of light. It heals and washes away the burdens and grief of the world. You have a choice. Approach the river and release whatever grief, anger, and sadness you have carried, or leave the journey.

Continuing, you follow the Priestess to the river of light. There, you release your grief through words, gestures, or sounds. Take a deep breath and let it flow into the running water as you exhale. Watch it float away and dissolve. Feel the clearing and release. (Pause)

Once you have finished, the Priestess hands you an object for your journey ahead. Examine the gift, and ask her any questions. (Pause)

As you finish, the Priestess speaks words of power to you and helps to ground you back into your body. She reminds you not to fear grief or sadness. Let it move through you and show you how to live well. (Pause)

Thank the Priestess with an offering, rise, and make your way from the stone circle back along the path to where you began and into your body. Gently return to the room and open your eyes.

Melpomene's Well-Wishes

"Initiate, if you encounter grief or tragedy, you may return to my realm and the heart's inner chamber. I have one more offering. Sit comfortably and receive. This is my blessing to you."

Take rest in me, dear one
The heavy load of long days and nights

Take rest in me, dear love
When the tears are endless sights

Take rest in me, dear one
When it's hard to see the light

Take rest in me, dear love
I bless your return to the living
at dawn's light.

With this, and many blessings to all,
Melpomene

Chapter VII
Erato: Muse of Erotic Poetry
& Romance

"The body sings with desire, and the soul answers in a chorus of longing." —Sappho

ELLA, THE WAYFINDER, AND I HAD BEEN WALKING FOR CLOSE TO TWO HOURS.

"Are we close?"

She smirked, "Hard to tell."

"Why is the door to Erato so far?"

"Keep asking the question."

Sigh.

Soon, hints of rose and jasmine permeated the Hall. *We're close,* I thought.

Ella tapped my arm. "Look," she said. The rose petals on the ground increased in number the farther we walked, culminating at a polished red door with no handle. I was bewildered.

"How do I unlock the door?"

"Oh, you'll need this," Ella said, handing me a key card. Wryly, I took it. The magenta card was inscribed with my name. "This will be fascinating," I murmured under my breath.

Ella grinned, "I will be waiting for your return."

"Who says I am coming back?"

As customary, I knocked and held my key card to the door handle. A chime rang, and the door clicked. I pushed inward. The scent was even more potent and enchanting. The petals continued into a plush, candle-lit room. The comforts of rugs, pillows, and a long table displaying wild grapes, figs, dates, red wine, and chocolate confections. The treats looked delicious, but where is Erato?

Singing drifted from a nearby room and guided me around a corner. Erato, in her beautiful red regalia, was applying scented oils to her neck and arms. She gleamed with warmth. "Hello, Initiate. Why has it taken you so long to visit me?"

I rubbed my arms and crossed them. "Fear, healing, and some avoidance?" As I announced each word, a blush crept behind my neck as my pulse quickened.

"I like your authenticity." She said, moving closer.

"I carry the golden arrow that pierces the heart of the most stubborn and wear the wild rose of allure and enchantment. Why do you fear pleasure, joy, and ecstasy, my love? They are your birthright.

I am the movement of the heart's desire and ecstasy. When I am near, one's passionate fire ignites the soul, engaging you in expanded bliss. You transform and experience beauty in the simplest moments. Your senses awaken, revealing the depths of your truest self.

Why do you not allow ecstasy within? Your senses, abundant with desires, are a gateway to a profoundly creative, embodied existence. Gaea molds your body with your intention, and the elements nourish you. The air caresses your skin, the alluring divine fire burns in your eyes, and the sweetest water pours throughout your body. The matter cradles and gently embraces you.

The realm of sensual and sexual desire is a place of women's mysteries. Yet many experience their sexual nature lying dormant and restricted. Much like creativity and magic, your sexual nature, even in its most acceptable forms, has been silenced. This part of the human experience sparks a regenerative nature and potency. Perhaps it is one reason why intimacy and sexual expression have been repressed and controlled for thousands of years.

Love is fuel for creativity. Engaging the senses adds depth to creative work, and love adds the flames of inspiration. Sexual energy is a powerful force and transformer; when channeled in an aligned way, passion removes the barriers.

As a Muse of love poetry, my passion rekindles and inspires through bliss, joy, and romance through continuous surrender. This unfolding, unwavering Divine Love story is at the core of life.

Come to the table. Can you recognize inside what delights you? Tell me what entices you and your fears of love, Beloved One. You have already taken the step to unlock the door. Whisper to me your heart's desire. The magic of love is all around you. What keeps you from surrendering to the fire of Divine Love. Why do you keep her from penetrating your heart? Does your body resist its breath? How long can you resist your truth?"

The Source of Love

Erato taps the cushion. "Come, sit beside me. I have a story of love to tell."

Part I – Into the Heart of Love

In my early years, I long wished to see my parents together. My mother loved Zeus with every aspect of her being, but he left after my sisters and I were born. Her love for him was unspoken, unmet, and unfulfilled.

"Our chemistry is off the scales, or he'll be back!" she insisted.

Many times, I found her alone, adrift in a sea of memories. She often stood at the window, waiting for their reunion. My sisters and I would catch her gazing skyward, watching for a forming cloud, and rushing outside when winds gust. Sculptures of Zeus appeared throughout the house. She refreshed his favorite flowers each day and kept a few thunderbolts sealed in a jar on the shelf. I lifted the jar, mesmerized, watching the whirling current spin in all directions. Was this love—a bottled-up keepsake?

Mother was happy with her Divine Beloved, even in his absence. I desired to experience that kind of connection, open-heartedness, and love toward everyone. But as my awareness deepened, an unseen barrier became apparent. An obstacle existed between love and the senses, blocking the Divine and separating humans from one another. That barrier was ego. As the eons passed, I watched its vine grow thick and unyielding.

I was conflicted. Mortals have free will. If only they understood that fear would dissolve the moment they tasted Eros. Had most of humanity chosen love, the world might look very different. Peculiar because, by nature, humans are hardwired for passion, love, and pleasure. Still, it's not too late.

So, I went into the world, attempting to arouse the fire of love, desire, and romance. I came to learn that many of the desires humans chase are seen through a distorted mirror. If that mirror were clear, they would realize their genuine wish is to reunite with themselves. For when you follow your cravings to their roots, you find they all point, ultimately, to the Divine. But what poetic words could I use to inspire such longing in a person?

Many were not accepting of these Mysteries or the power of their sexual and erotic energy. You've somehow forgotten that you are born of desire. It is a desire that moves you to create, unite, give birth, and fall in love. Love urges one to move beyond blocks, beliefs, and wounds. It purifies. You can imagine my frustration with the contradictions. I learned that not everyone longs for their true self.

Through the years, I have inspired many to reawaken their desires from pain and slumber. I have kissed fire into the mouths of poets, who quenched their thirst by writing pages of passion. I have loosened the buttons to the way of the heart in many artists, whose souls bear it all with every brushstroke. Nothing delights the Muse more than picking ripe fruit, ready in its sweet surrender.

Erato leaned back on the cushion. My journey with love continues as the world learns to move beyond its separation. But let me tell you how I became Erato, the Muse of Erotic Poetry.

Every story or poem begins with a Muse who inspires a desire within us to take action. My action was to experience ecstasy and love in its purest form and bring it to the world. It was ages ago when I yearned to show humanity the path to love, to inspire songs and words of ecstasy. This naïve, bold pursuit and its unrelenting longing required a journey to the one place few Gods ever ventured: the heart of the Void, into emptiness itself, a powerful place from which all of life emerges. Without a doubt, I believed this was where love was at its purest, most potent form. As for the recipe and elixir of love, I had planned to speak to the Fates.

For this journey, I prepared myself with this body and spirit to withstand the power I was about to enter. I spent time in nature and was careful not to indulge in too many delectables. Months passed until I felt ready. On the day of my departure, I told my family I'd be resting for a few months in the sunnier south and wasn't sure how long I'd be gone. Since I did this from time to time, they thought nothing of it. Mother would never have allowed me to visit the Void alone, and I didn't want her to worry. I left home in the early morning as winter gave way to spring. The voyage was long, and it took time to find the Void.

Before me swirled an infinite darkness unlike anything else in space or time. It felt raw and limitless, an ocean of mist, humming and vibrating with the sound of spirit. Setting my intention at the edge, I leaped into its vast emptiness. A current-like tide lifted me. Nothingness wrapped itself around my body and held me. It showed me that it was all things. Love permeated me in all aspects of its oneness. Barriers within the mind fell away. I surrendered to the pure, loving presence beyond words, shifting my parts into wholeness. Quiet. And one.

It's unclear how much time passed; it may have been a second or a year. When I reawakened, the pulse of my senses contracted, and my muscles convulsed. The bliss was so immense it seized me. I moaned and morphed as renewal surged through me. A magnetism spread across my body, and my eyes illuminated transcendent fire. The mist of the Void carried me across its threshold and birthed me anew.

Part II – Fate & Love

At the outskirts of space, far from the Olympians, resides the Temple of the Fates. I arrived following a vast cosmic river of stars. The waterway led to a staircase that ascended into a lush, ancient forest; as I climbed past the grand pillars of light, the temple and plaza teemed with life. Some spun threads, while others washed and hung fabric. In the distance stood the Tree of Life, towering over a celestial courtyard. This place retains the delicate threads, geometries, and patterns that shape the structure of life. Three wise sisters, seers, and fates are the wisdom keepers of all timelines. I believed they would hold the elixir of love, a charm to guide all humans back to each other and themselves.

As I ascended the stairs, a Fate awaited me. It was Atropos, my Godparent. I'm sure she sensed my presence long before my arrival.

"Dedicated one of Love, welcome to the Cosmic Temple. I caught the light of your arrival last week. You've been on quite an epic journey! We would have had a larger ceremony, but things have been hectic. Still, I'm glad you found time to visit the place!"

Atropos towered in height, like most primordials, and was impossible to miss, even among the trees. But it was her irises, so bright and radiant that they were indistinguishable from the whites of her eyes. She was elegant, with long silver stands flowing to her hips and wisdom pouring from her voice. When I reached the top, she gathered me in her arms, like a mother reunited with her child after a long trip.

"This place is even more stunning than I could have ever imagined, far beyond what I had dreamed. The tree is ten times larger than you described, Atropos!"

The wise one pointed. "Long before time began, the Tree of Life summoned us. Well, that's what it feels like, anyway. As the Fates, the tree entrusted us with the sacred responsibility of being the protectors and guardians of life. Every few thousand years, we've added to the forest, temple, and gardens. Come, let me show you the interior."

As I followed her inside, a mighty solar wind blew. Atropos stopped. I watched her eyes grow brighter as if she were tuning into the tree and the One Source. After a few seconds, she spoke. "Another massive change is upon us, Erato. We've been aware of the great wave coming, and that's why things have been so chaotic."

We watched as the Tree of Life radiated like a star, its providence pulsating through the roots and flowing into the river below. We moved deeper into the inner sanctuary. I noticed the high vaulted ceilings and clear quartz crystal windows. A room filled with hundreds of chairs around a wooden table lit from underneath.

"I thought you three determined the fate of birth, life, and death?"

"Yes, we do, but as a wise one sees, many possibilities exist. You must recognize that the universe has its destiny, and we are all involved in the play of life. Come, I want to show you another room."

We crossed the sanctuary and passed through the hall into a small study. On the far side of the room, a Goddess sat immersed in her writing. Moonlight streamed through the window, mingling over her skin.

"Do you remember Lachesis? She visited your home a few times. She's the Fate who determines the events of a lifetime, like this meeting." Atropos had a twinkle in her eye.

Lachesis was captivating. I could feel her heartbeat and magnetic presence clear across the room. She was a goddess with long, dark locks naturally falling over her breasts and eyes that shone with the same illumination as Atropos'. Lachesis peered at us from her book, and our gazes met. She pushed back her chair, standing to greet us. I was mesmerized by the way she sauntered. Her upturned bow-lips parted as she moved toward me; time seemed to shift, and my spirit quickened. This woman exuded enough sexual lifeforce to keep the cosmos forever spinning.

"Sister, you remember Erato."

"Of course!" Lachesis said, moving in for a hug. Our bodies met, and an electric charge jolted me so powerfully I was breathless. I wondered if the lingering vibrations were the Void, but this felt different. It was alive.

"I have work to attend to, Lachesis. Are you willing to show Erato the rest of the temple grounds?"

"Yes, I'd love to give her a tour," she said, her voice warm and inviting. She touched my arm, drawing me closer.

As Atropos left, I turned to Lachesis. "I need to tell you, I don't remember you at the house."

"It was long ago, Erato, but a few times we stopped by and found you gone. You were visiting the sun in the South. You must be hungry. I can show you to the dining area. If I recall, you like strawberries."

Following a quick snack, Lachesis showed me the sanctuary of light, a spacious room with walls composed of amethyst crystals. I felt bathed and wrapped in its softness and calm essence. "This is our healing space at the temple, and it's the oldest room. Let's venture through the astral pathway to the western gardens, to one of my favorite places."

We traveled through a starry tunnel twinkling with distant stars, swirling nebulas, and planets far beyond reach. Fire and ice embraced colors of light and dark, a full display of the celestial mysteries unfolding, creating, and expanding.

The path of starlight began to merge with deep green foliage. Fig trees were heavy with fruit and bent low in welcome. Plucking a ripe one, it felt warm to the touch, its skin tender and rich with nectar. As I bit into it, sweet honey flooded my senses and burst onto my tongue.

Lachesis beamed. "Come and see the roses."

Past the figs and beyond the hedges was another green passage. Lachesis took out her key and unlocked the gate. "This is one of my favorite spots besides the moon garden."

As I crossed the threshold, the alluring scent of sweet roses filled the air and enchanted me. My whole body buzzed for each flower. Lachesis had planted an array of varieties. Rambling roses climbed the distant wall overlooking a reflecting pool with a sculpted-winged fountain. To the sides, clusters of blooms dabbed with pinks, whites, and reds were set in front of natural arched trellises.

"This is my first planting, Rosa Damascena. I especially love the dark pink hues of this variety; its blooming cycle is longer."

Lachesis cupped one of the fully bloomed roses. "Can you recognize the fragrant notes of this one?"

I drew my face close to the soft, velvety petals, inhaling its intoxicating essence.

"It has a fruity citrus note."

"Yes, and…"

"A spicy cinnamon warmth?"

Lachesis leaned in, staring at my lips. "Yes, keep going…"

I trembled, and my words slowed. "Undertones of—ah, a sensual musk… sandalwood."

Lachesis inched her alluring body closer; her eyes held mine. I felt her fingers sweep my hair aside, sending flutters through me. She whispered in my ear with her delicious voice.

"Yes, you are so good at this, Erato."

I pressed my lips together, and my breath deepened. Lachesis lingered as our cheeks touched. Her arm wrapped around my waist. I could feel both our longing.

"Did you notice the floral sweetness, Erato?"

"Yes, Lachesis," I whispered.

She traced my bottom lip with her finger, then pressed her lips to mine. A passion of electric fire ignited me, and my pulse pounded. I kissed her more urgently, and the embrace deepened. At that moment, existence disappeared. There was nothing except the heat of our connection and the infinite. Lachesis gently pulled back, smiled, and took my hand. "Come, let me show you the Tree of Life."

Part III – Golden Arrow of Transformation

Fate pulled us ever nearer. Countless evenings, I found myself on Lachesis' balcony of dreams. After a long day of weaving destinies, she would retreat to her inner chamber, and I would softly kiss and caress her tenderly.

One such evening, she led me to a higher realm of love and longing. In a sacred space of pure Goddess essence, she activated me. With deep exultation, she held a golden, luminous arrow.

"Erato, you came for the elixir of love to heal humanity. All Beings contain states of joy, love, and bliss. To reach them, you must remove the blockages causing the illusion. Do you trust me?"

"Yes." I felt the room's vibration elevate.

She pressed the tip of the arrow gently against the center of my chest. An explosive crack of lightning rang out. I fell back in slow motion, and my vision blurred. Ecstatic energy filled me with joy and pleasure, love expanded, and bliss ascended. I felt the Void's familiar emptiness and life's vivid, sensual nature unite, awakening, and transforming me. I fell to my knees in complete surrender and rose that night as Erato, Poet of Love.

Curiosity stirred in me. *Did Lachesis have a hand in our meeting?*

"Yes," she said, "I foresaw our meeting, but it was also the will of the One. Love and Fate had to intertwine. When you open to love, you open to all of creation."

She traced her fingers through my thick curls as we lay together in bed. Lachesis smiled, her eyes satisfied. "A divine happenstance," she whispered.

"It was at this point when my work began, offering the roses of allure to those fated to meet, piercing the hearts of those longing and ready for the Beloved. Our love story continues." Erato smiled.

About Sappho

These lips kissed her hand
her shoulder, her neck
A longing to be freed
in sweetness of senses

Pierced by her eyes
her heart, her bow 'n arrow
Beyond day and night
in the realm of Erato

Enchanted whispers
her desires, her delights
With tease and yearning
in breath and burning

Drenched in her scent
her hair, her thighs
Completely mesmerized
in sensual singing cries

Embrace of ecstasy
her breath, her pleasure
My heart fully undone
in total surrender

Journey to the Rose Sanctuary

"I invite you to find a comfortable position. You will soon meet one of the Priestesses of Love Poetry. She will be your guide," said Erato.

Notice your body sinking further into the floor or soft cushions. Begin to take a deep breath in and out a few times. Looking toward your eyebrows, close your eyelids, take another deep breath, and relax further into the body. Relax as you let go more and more and start to feel the heat of the sun upon you and the faint smell of floral sweetness around you. As you drift further into the sweetness, begin to sense yourself standing by an enchanting turquoise river. Feel your toes tickled by the soft moss beneath your feet. Feel the vibrant aliveness of the water and listen to it bubble across stones and soil. The water calls and invites you to restore yourself. If you're comfortable, undress and ease into the river. Let it cleanse and purify you. (Pause)

Finishing, thank the river with an offering and retrieve your clothes and dress. Your eyes trace the river flowing down from a source upon a hill. The luscious moss path below your feet marks the way. As you ascend, notice what flowers and animals are nearby. (Pause)

At the top is a spring of turquoise water with blooming roses of varieties and colors. The fragrance compels your senses. As you journey closer, you notice an arched floral entryway. Feel the breeze across your skin, inviting you through. Inside, a lavish rose garden with groups of people sitting in circles, some reading to one another and others laughing with delight. In the center sits a woman casually leaning on soft pillows; a loose robe drapes over her body. The Priestess's full lips moved with intention as she read aloud to a small group. As she finishes, the group progresses to another part of the garden. Two women strolling by tell you the Priestess wants to speak with you. Venturing down the pathway toward her, you start to feel a pleasure welling up and intoxication. The mixture of flowers and a magical atmosphere expands you with joy. As you near, her turquoise eyes recognize every met and unmet desire within you. She stands as you approach.

"Elated to see you made it," she says. The potent scent of rose mixed with jasmine saturates you. She leans into you and whispers in your ear, "Tell me what you have learned of love, desire, and pleasure. Have you felt the wisdom of the heart?" Sit and take your time sharing with her what you have learned. (Pause)

After finishing the conversation, she offers you her hand and leads you to a hedge with a door. "Through this passage, you will reach a place where you can remove the blocks and barriers to love, desire, and your sensual, erotic self. With your creative key in hand, you are safe and protected. It will show you the way. I will wait for you. When you are ready, open the door and enter. (Pause)

Begin to finish up and make your way back through the door. (Pause)

Once you return to the Priestess, ask her questions to clarify what you have found. (Pause)

The Priestess tells you that your time is coming to a close. She has one final gift for you if you are willing to accept and consent. If you choose to leave, another Priestess will guide you to the south garden gate. Once entering, you return to the room with your body.

If you prefer to continue, simply tell the Priestess yes. The Priestess lifts her left hand, filled with rose petals, and blows them energetically onto your body. For "self-love," she says, gathering a few more petals and pressing them gently against your heart. She then traces honeyed oil across your lips. "To speak with beauty and sweetness". The honey lingers, heightening your senses. She whispers in your ear, "You are worthy of pleasure. You deserve joy and happiness. You are love."

The Priestess finishes, and you thank her, leaving an offering of gratitude. Two women arrive to escort you to the south garden gate. As you walk through, you find yourself standing on the moss by the stream where you started. Take a few deep breaths and come back to the room and your body.

Erato's Well-Wish

"I lovingly leave you these words, Initiate. Allow them to sink into you and kiss open your heart. If you feel comfortable, relax into my arms."

Open your gate to me—let me bloom your wondrous garden

Open your door to me—let me give you nourishment and sweetness

Open your house to me—let me light a Divine fire and spark of Spirit

Open your bed to me—let me kiss the wounds and free your passions

Open your eyes to me—let me reflect back one's true love and embrace

In this place is where your cup fills with life again…

All my love,
Erato

Chapter VIII
Euterpe: Muse of Music

"In music, the spirit of the Gods finds its voice, and through it, we are connected to the divine." —Pythagoras

I PLACED THE KEY CARD IN MY POCKET FOR SAFEKEEPING.

"I'm back!"

"You're brimming over," said Ella.

I blushed. "Okay, where to next?"

"We've arrived."

"What?"

She tossed me a pair of sunglasses, slid on her own, and glided across the Hall to a portal radiating like the sun.

"So, these two doors are next to each other?"

"Yes, these two Muses are closely linked in your case," Ella assured me.

"Is this common?"

"Sometimes two Muses partly overlap for a person, so neither common nor rare," Ella admitted.

"Why is this portal so bright?"

Ella cleared her throat, adjusted her glasses, and swept her blonde bangs. "Time to get started."

With a swift motion, I knocked and entered. The gold handle was hot. The sound of a cello's haunting, deep tones hung in the air. I half expected something like a beach, but the recital hall was pleasant. Euterpe motioned for me to sit, then placed the cello in my hands. I skimmed over the music. It was alive as if divinely orchestrated.

Was this fifth-dimensional?

She must have heard my thoughts. Like a proper music teacher, she began her monologue.

"Close your eyes. Let the sound dance through you. Allow each part of you to resonate with the shifting notes and tones. Let them draw deep rhythms, harmonies, and abstract colors in and around you. Release into the sound. Play the song you are here to bring into the world. Find the bridge of harmony to your heart. Find the connection, the expansion, within the sound of life. Let each movement fill you."

I listened, mentally taking notes.

"Relax. You are overcomplicating what stirs within you. Let it move through you into the instrument to give it life. Allow the music to carry the emotions through you and heal. This power creates a magic that shifts the patterns of the world." Noticing my confusion, Euterpe stopped and pulled a chair to sit beside me. "Okay, let's start from the beginning."

"As a Muse, I engage, inspire, and awaken your inner music, calling it forth to share with the world. Musicians are sacred pattern keepers, the givers of change and culture. You were born from sound, which is why it affects you so profoundly. It touches all Beings. Sound penetrates the physical and extends beyond the mind's comprehension. It is not a simple language to explain in words. Music was born at the inception of the universe and continues its mantra of life. It exists in the backdrop, waiting for a string or voice to resonate with its vibration. Alongside music exists its complementary companion, silence.

You are a vibration that emerges from the sound of creation. Your form is a frequency of the past and the future. When there is discord, music realigns what is out of tune. Striking a sound on the outer plane shifts the inner one. Within music lives nature and the elements: the air of the lungs and spirit; the water of receptivity and the power of emotions; the fire, the spark of inspiration, motivation, and ecstasy; and earth, the body, and the materials that create the instrument. By combining the elements with sound, the wise bring powerful change, reshaping the world. Adept musicians have raised tsunamis, moved mountains, built cities, spun galaxies across the universe, and channeled spirit into form. Music is alchemical, a key that unlocks and transcends the gates of the subconscious, sparking transformation."

The Breath of Music

Initiate, close your eyes, and listen to this tale.

Part I – The Dream of Music

Long before the development of words, music formed us. Heart-walkers and dreamers sang with the flute. They called to the Earth, Gods, and Goddesses. Hollowed-out bones, crafted by avian songwriters, expressed the body's breath of life, purity, and spirit. The flute mimics the essence of how spirit and inspiration traverse through the body. It is revealing that the origin of music begins with the way the human vessel expresses itself.

At first, the strike, rhythm, and action of the drum, cymbal, and gong procured ritual, healing, and communication with the Spirits and ancestors. With time, wind and percussion gave way to the early strings of lyres and forged bronze-shaped trumpets. The ancients sang with vowels and incantations, with intentions traveling on notes that connected thought, songs to alter states of being, attuned to moving through the stuck places or manifesting new realities.

The world shifted again in complexity, and intricate forms like piano, violin, and clarinet emerged. The industrial age brought a refinement of machinery, creating the saxophone and accordion. In humanity's future, electrifying frequencies synthesized through instruments will produce a sound fusion with the elements, alchemy of scales, and the subtle sounds of nature, renewing forces of harmonic resonance. Each age and epoch expresses itself through music, revealing the story of where human consciousness and innovation reside.

As a Muse, I acknowledge that music from instruments or singing creates a gate to the Mysteries. The repetitive nature of beats communicates with the subconscious, guiding you into states of healing, transformation, and movement, awakening different centers in the mind and body. Music naturally leads you into a trance, taking you beyond the mundane and evoking an ecstatic state in the body.

I have influenced many bard-walkers to play music with sacred intent. As one's senses ripen inward, the higher self awakens. The more embodied a musician is, the more the music stirs and channels lifeforce, weaving connections and shifting atmospheres. At its core, music nourishes and awakens the heart and soul of the world.

Part II – Music, born from Muse

Euterpe crossed the room to get a glass of water. "Thirsty?"

"Yes," I said. *Who wouldn't accept a drink from a Muse?*

With the glasses, she strolled over, handed me one, and sat.

"So, how did you become the Muse of Music?" I asked.

"Yes, I remember the story clearly. It was like any other ordinary day, yet unforgettable. It may have manifested from my deep yearning for harmony between the Gods and mortals."

"Unlike my sisters, I did not speak, at least not right away. Much of my early awareness was shaped by watching and witnessing life unfold. As the strangest of the Muse sisters, I wasn't as emphatic about things as the rest of the family. I enjoyed listening to the sunrise or the morning rain touching arid leaves. Silence was my friend. It helped me sense the things most overlooked. Sitting peacefully, I felt and heard the vibrations of distant stars and the movement of far-off fields. In a complementary way, silence brought me to music."

Once, on a day like any other, I sat listening to the sacred Pineios River far below in the Tempe Valley of ancient Greece. Beyond the passing sound of water, a group of warblers chirped on a branch and trilled at the ground. Sweeping my hand through the high grass, I uncovered a large bird carcass. With respect, I placed the bones on a rock and began to dig. The evening breeze began to intensify. Hearing a sharp sound from the direction of the bones, I stopped. As the wind sent another breath, the hollow bones started to speak. The elements shifted its song, altering its pitch and melody. I carved small holes to guide the flow of air and, through my touch, infused it with the spirit of the Muse.

After playing the bones with a few attempts, notes rang throughout the forest, and the firmament filled with enchantment. The birds flew closer, deer jumped, and foxes scurried forth in fascination. Zephyros sprinted through the wild grasses, meowed, and bolted straight into my arms; he smelled the instrument approvingly and tucked his head under my chin.

I found the precise distance and frequency of the instrument after months of trials. I played three clear notes by the river. The water bubbled, the clouds parted, and the trees tipped. Inside, I sensed a power emerging. Peculiar symbols sprang from the bones, forming a circle over the river, attracting the wind and water, and converging into a symphony of elements and sound. Growing in power, it circulated and expanded into the landscape, lifting me.

The brilliance covered my body and enveloped me in waves of vibrations. Sparks lit my skin, and power flashed from my fingertips. My throat burned with heat, a sharp pressure pressed against my temples, and the pain surged through blockages in my joints and hands. I focused, attempting to surrender to the sensations. The symbols imprinted themselves into my mind. The tension swelled, and the momentum kept building; I thought it would tear me apart as a scream clawed at my throat. Then, the pressure subsided and set me back to the ground. Sparks arched over the instrument and across my fingers, unlocking some greater force from within.

A new language merged into the world, music.

Part III – Finding Her Voice

For years, I passed on the gift of music and its transformational properties. Music comes from the soul of the Muse. It is of us and the natural world. As I integrated, I recognized this was my part to play in humankind's seasons: to bring healing, connection, and unseen patterns through vibrating language, to facilitate the bypass of the egoic grasp, and to create unity. I passed on the gift of music into the world's fabric early on, but one place stands out. Like countless others, I met an abandoned woman with large, dark, curious eyes in a peaceful, nomad village.

I have to admit, it was actually Zephyros who found her. He had been acting ornery all morning, choosing to roam across a fabric overhang to eye the merchant fare. Motivated by food, Zephyros ignored my pleas.

"Zephye! Zephyeee!"

He licked his paw, then stared at the vendor, and finally turned to me.

"Zephye, don't you dare. Don't! I know what you're thinking!"

He was eyeing the salmon, preparing to jump right over an older man tending his shop. I held my breath.

To my relief, he leaped to the side and landed straight into the woman's arms. She was sitting against a building, lost in her own world. Caught off guard, she gathered him up and looked around, trying to figure out where he came from. Loving the attention, he snuggled into her and promptly conked out for a nap. The brunette woman tucked him in close. I knew I should trust anyone Zephyros found, someone receptive to music and the Muse.

"Hi. I'm Euterpe. You found my cat."

Nervously, she pulled him closer.

"His name is Zephyros. You're safe with him. What is your name? Are you okay?"

She shook her head, touched her belly, and gestured to her mouth.

"You're hungry?"

She nodded fervently. I hesitated. *Where was her family?* My inner senses told me she was also unable to speak, a lump formed in the back of my throat. We crossed to a merchant selling sticks of salmon, roots, and various treats. Even as she ate, she didn't let go of Zephyros; instead, she fed him pieces of her food. I asked her about her family, but her essence dimmed every time I spoke about them, and her eyes lowered. While talking, I noticed the woman stop to watch a group of warblers singing. She tried to chirp to communicate with them. I sensed she wanted to reconnect with her own voice.

Behind the vendor's table were discarded bones. I plucked two, tied them together, and added a few holes. Discreetly, I conjured sparks from my fingertips, animating the instrument to life. I infused it with the primal forces of the elements, light patterns, and the essence of the Muse. Whoever plays such an instrument in an aligned way can transform and re-enchant the world.

After a hearty meal, the three of us took the north road to an open field. I stopped, took out the newly charged instrument, and played a few notes.

"I call it an aulos."

She was mesmerized. I handed her the instrument and demonstrated how to produce a sound.

"SCREEeeechhhh, FFFFffffffff!" She grimaced. Zephyros' fur bristled. My eyes squinted. The first sound was horrendous, as was the second and the third. Mortals, I reminded myself, were unfamiliar with such instruments. She wasn't yet open enough to allow the full inspiration to flow through her. But despite the rough start, she was intrigued and excited. That's when I knew I'd take her under my wing, guiding her until she could play in her way.

After four seasons of practice, we traveled northeast for several days and arrived at a sacred well I had enhanced long ago with my sisters.

"We will rest here. Put your things down." I swept her body with rosemary and thyme sprigs. The fragrance grounded us, pulling us back to our center. Taking out my aulos, I summoned the veil to part, revealing the Spring of the Muse.

"When you're ready, sip from the spring."

The young woman reached into the crystalline water and drank. After the third and final sip, a forceful cough wracked her body. Her hand flew to her throat, and her voice trembled. "What is this?"

Her eyes widened, unrecognizing the sound. She had not spoken since childhood.

"You are finding your voice," I said.

She glared at me, a mix of shock, curiosity, and fear, as her world shifted. As the water integrated and traced through her, she spoke.

"My name is Charis (Χάρις). I am from the north, from the highlands and ice." Tears rolled down her cheeks. How long had it been since she had heard her own name?

Zephyros brushed against her leg and purred. She reached down and patted his head. She then took out her instrument and began to play a melody unlike any other. The world listened; the water sang, the moon brightened, and the crickets joined in rhythm. Evening flowers bloomed in rapture as twilight lay gently at her feet. As the last note echoed through the land, she glowed, amazed at the magic she had woven.

"I can feel all of life vibrating," Charis said.

"It is the inspiration and ecstatic elation of spirit," I said. "It's been within you all along. The breath of life has brought you back to yourself."

Musical Nature

Past the lips, breath, and wind
A call to the east
A call to the south
A call to the west and north
A call to Spirit and Goddesses

The voice of stars
The clap of wings
The footsteps of humans
The burbling of water
The strike of thunder
The wisp of trees
The scratches and taps of squirrels
The caw and chirp of crows
The quiet pause of snowy fields

A symphony of communication
Vibrating the air
Seizing the ear
Entrancing the mind

Nature's instruments
Playing the sound of life

Journey to Voice of Expression

You and Euterpe enter through a garden door. *"Let us sit outside while I take you on this journey, Initiate. You are about to meet an ancient Priestess of music and sound."*

Move into a comfortable position. Notice your body, and breathe deeply in and out a few times. Breathe deeper, sinking further into your body. Bring your awareness to all the sounds around you. Notice which sounds become more apparent and louder. Merge deeper into the sounds and allow your inner landscape to shift into a bright meadow. Know as you enter this journey, you are safe. See, hear, smell, and feel the wind feathering each leaf and flower. Hear it whistling through your hair.

In the distance, songbirds sing out to life. Listen. Begin to feel the ground under your feet and see the birds flying overhead. One of them flies and rests on your shoulder. It will show you which path to take. Note what kind of bird greets you. (Pause)

With each step, faint and distant music gets louder. Do you sense or feel what type of music is playing? As you venture further up the path, you will see an amphitheater. An ensemble is playing music. Is it familiar? As you get closer, an instrument is sitting off to one side. The Priestess waves and invites you to start playing. You may be surprised at how naturally it comes to you. Notice whether you are by yourself or in a group. (Pause)

Allow yourself to merge more deeply with the music and notice which part of you resonates with it. Feel and listen as the patterns weave through you. What does it reveal? (Pause)

Ask the Priestess why you chose this particular instrument. What is it telling you about life, creativity, and healing? Continue to ask questions and absorb the messages. (Pause)

When you are ready, the Priestess will guide you to a door. Here, you will find your unique, expressive voice, the one you may have been unknowingly searching for. With your creative key, open the door and enter. Find your voice and bring it back with you. (Pause)

Start to finish and make your way back to the door that is being held for you. The Priestess greets you with your instrument. She hands you one final gift for the coming months. Ask her any questions you may have about your voice or her gift. (Pause)

The Priestess gently informs you that it is time to return. Offer her a token of gratitude. As you do, she reminds you to integrate all that you have experienced. If you feel called, take the musical instrument and bring it back with you as part of your journey. Then, with your winged friend by your side, retrace the path you came. Returning to the bright meadow. When you're ready, gently come back to the room and into your body.

A Well-Wish from Euterpe

"Initiate, I leave you with a well-wish for your journey ahead, with and in the music of life. Relax into the sounds of my words."

May you live with a sensitive nature
So, it courses and plays through your body with resonates

May your hands be blessed with music and create
So it may touch and heal all whom you carry dear

May you hear the true song of a lover
So their whispers may amplify your spirit

May you feel and let in the vibration of life with your heart
So it may attune you to even greater love

Well-wishes to you Initiate,
Euterpe

Chapter IX
Terpsichore: Muse of Dance

"The soul of the dancer is found in the rhythm of the movement."
—Anonymous

CLOSING THE ILLUMINATED DOOR BEHIND ME, I SCANNED THE HALL FOR ELLA.

The Wayfinder was nowhere to be found. A piece of paper on the door caught my eye.

> *"Initiate, I'm in rest and restoration. You must guide your-self to Terpsichore. Over —>*
> *Trust your intuition to show you the way."*

Crunching up the paper, I placed it in my pocket. *Right, I'm on my own.* Sigh.

I felt a tug toward the south, and the Hall felt animated. "Okay, Hall, please reveal the way to the Muse of Dance."

As I made my way, my body grew warmer. Veering to the right, I heard faint sounds like a tap dancer and paused at an orange door with spiral details. Was this Terpsichore's entry? My anxiety started to kick in. What happens if I wander into the wrong room? For good measure, I glanced at the next door over; nothing. I tapped and walked through the entryway.

Inside, the room was expansive, with a wooden floor and quartz walls. Above, a tapestry of stars. On the far side, a Priestess and dancers emerged through an archway. I could feel the ancient drums playing in the background. Each dancer wore a large hat and white attire and spun like whirling dervishes. Inviting the Divine, their movements mirrored the epic power of the cosmos. The drumbeats amplified, and the Muse, Terpsichore, entered the room. She moved gracefully across the floor, and the whirlers pivoted to the side. Even from afar, I felt her gaze piercing into me.

"Place your hands in mine, and let me show you the dance of life beyond the veil of the mundane. Let this dance fill you with ecstasy and the abundant Nature of the universe. Close your eyes. Let the drum move through you. Allow every part of you to resonate with the shifting tones. Let it call you to your essence.

The life within you is a continuous symphony guiding you to its conclusion. How will you dance to the crescendo of your life? To each breath? Life lives in the movements. Your body is a sculpture designed from the tears and laughter of countless ancestors. Made from the sun, moon, and stars, it is a continuous vibration of your Beingness and everlasting cycle. A subtle body and universe embracing flesh as a vessel.

How will you dance to the song of love, beauty, and devotion? Embody the Divine, merge in sacred union with your body. Step into the joys and through the sorrows into who you are meant to become. A stagnant life is one unlived, unengaged, and more dangerous than any poison or ill wishes.

Allow yourself to soar above the landscape of your undoing to an incarnation of fiery truth. With gesture, with excitement, with expansion, ignite the inner room of yourself. Claim your embodiment. Claim your creative nature. Dance the moment of a lifetime."

Finding the Dance

Grace," Terpsichore said, "let me speak of my story. Though it is not an easy one to tell, at its core, it is a story of freedom.

Part I – The Enchanting Magi

Once, before the great walls and many boundaries of kingdoms stood, before the sea rose, in the age of the first writings, when magic was wielded, and fantastic Beings roamed the lands by steed, a small group of Magi were visiting the high plateau. People of knowledge, recognized by their towering golden hats, were known far and wide. They were the keepers of ancient relics and priceless wisdom. They held secrets and magic unlike our own.

Their fellowship drifted throughout the world to uncharted lands, searching for forgotten knowledge and lost artifacts. They were said to be enchanted riders, each with impressive skill and agility. I knew little about them until a gust of wind changed my course. My sisters and I passed their convoy on our way east, and the one thing I had kept hidden prompted our encounter.

A procession of Magi traveled by us in the opposite direction, so I slowed, curious and captivated. Then, the breeze shifted without notice, and a great gust blew over us. I was unprepared for the unforeseen event that was about to unfold. My hood loosened and flew back, but before I could catch it, my fiery, wavy locks sprang free and flared out in all directions. Though we were all born with my mother's features, my hair was different, matching the constellation of freckles that blessed my face, in stark contrast to my large, dark eyes. It was rare at the time, and the reason I kept it covered was to avoid drawing attention from onlookers.

One of the Magi, the Shadowbearded One, saw me and abruptly stopped. The others pulled on their horses' reins, and the animals shuddered, kicked the ground, lowered their necks, and snorted. All of them focused on me.

I tried to tuck my tresses away from onlookers, but it was too late. The charming man asked, "What is your name?"

I did not answer.

Polyhymnia, discerning their magic, shifted her head and released a breath into the dust and wind. Within seconds, a great storm brewed, aiming sand over the road next to us. The light faded to night. Within a snap of a moment, my sisters and I were swept a great distance. Secure, we brushed ourselves off and proceeded to make a fire.

Klio, clutching an armful of sticks, walked by. "You must be more careful, sister."

"It was the Magi's doing, and it was wise you didn't tell him your name, Terpsichore," Polyhymnia stated.

"Yes, an enchantment was present. I'm surprised you didn't feel it, sister," Erato said to Klio.

With her usual distant expression, Urania unpacked the magical chest. "Those mortals were different."

Thalia chimed in, breaking the tension, "Could we find another way to travel? I have sand everywhere!" We laughed as she poured sand from her pocket into a pile that reached her knees.

After a few days, we made camp by a giant yew tree at the curve of a wide river. Calliope finished telling her last epic tale, and we cheered at its heroic ending. I lay watching the coals burn to a powdery gray, drifting into the dream realm and giving this Muse's body its rest.

I was jolted awake by rustling sounds at some point in the early morning. "Sisters?" I sprang from the covers to find myself in a wooden cart with a handful of Magi. My sisters were gone.

Not realizing I was awake, I frantically rushed to the edge of the cart and leaned over. A steep slope below offered my chance to lunge and break free. Whoosh. Zap! I bounced back by a mysterious field surrounding the cart.

"Hey, no use in escaping. This caravan is protected. Get down!" one of the Magi warned.

I sat, shaking, watching them cover a distance twice that of a normal human. What were they?

Their pace slowed. Ahead, a dozen full-size tents came into view, and along the rim of their settlement, torches with blue fire. As we approached, I saw the pale man, the Shadowbearded One, smiling at his arriving men and speaking briefly to them.

He headed toward the back of the cart, scanning to ensure I was unharmed. "So, you found my prize," he joked with his men. But then his tone turned cold, and his blue eyes narrowed. "Tell me, what is your name? Where did you come from?"

"I could ask the same question," I replied, not giving him the answer he was hoping for.

"So, we are at an impasse," he said.

He pointed to two of his men. "Lock her in with the Diwali relic."

From one cage to another, I sat for what felt like weeks. Occasionally, guards sent food scraps, but my hunger had faded. Where were my sisters? They were searching for me, right?

One evening, a guard retrieved me from the cage and escorted me to his tent. The heavy scent of musk filled the air. He was not in his standard riding attire but wore an open, sleek crimson robe, linen pants, and a gold cloth belt tied around his middle.

"So, are you ready to tell me your name?" he asked.

I said nothing.

He strutted over to pour wine. "I'll make you a deal. I'll answer your question, but you must answer one of mine."

"What creatures are you, demigods?" I asked, trying to keep my composure.

"Ha! No, we're not demigods. Would I be doing this for a living, collecting magical relics, if I were? We're humans of alchemy and magic, yes. We learned a technology passed down from those beyond the stars, other realms, and our ancestors. We've learned to harness power in the material world. The Magi keep this knowledge close."

"What is your name?" I boldly asked.

As I spoke, shouting erupted from the other side of the tent. A guard barged in. "Sir, a relic has been taken. We suspect one of the second men." He slammed his drink. "Damn it." He glared at me and came closer. The heat of his breath was on my skin, his nostrils flaring. He reached out and touched my hair. "I get to ask the next question."

"Clean her up, take her to suitable arrangements with finer food. She's underweight," the Shadowbeared One said to the guard as he left. I was brought to a new tent, this time with a place to sleep and a table full of fruit. Sinking onto the bed, I began to weep. "How am I going to get out of this situation?"

Part II – Filled with Earth & Sky

Hours went by, and my eyes grew heavy with exhaustion. As I dozed off, I heard an agonizing and chilling scream, followed by another and another. Fear alerted me. I ran over and peeled a tiny opening in the tent and saw several guards at the entry. "What is happening?"

"No need for alarm. A guard tried to return one of the sacred relics and was captured."

"What do you do with these relics?" I innocently asked.

"Some of them are sold for a price. Others are traded for favors. The most powerful ones are kept by the Magi," another guard said.

I was barely able to watch as they tied the wayward sentinel to a wooden post and repeatedly tortured him. The Shadowbearded One taking breaks of wine between lashes. With a mere thought, stones formed midair and crashed into the man's chest. Next, his hands formed fire and flame. The torture continued until the early morning. Where this courageous man once stood, only ashes.

I have never seen such horrible acts by a human. How can someone be this cruel? As one of the younger Muses, I gathered my sisters had kept things from me.

That night, instead of my typical slumber resting, one of the Fates appeared to me.

"Terpsichore, Terpsichore, TerPsiCHORE!"

"Yes!" I said, turning over. A glowing figure was hovering near my bed.

"Atropos! Please help, I am held in a camp by a group of Magi!"

"We gathered. We have been searching for you for weeks. Your sisters could not get a read on you and presumed magic was involved. Erato arrived asking for our help. Klio went to see the warrior goddess Athena to petition for support. For some reason, your signature essence is more potent."

"He must be tired, the one who is keeping me. He was busy all night torturing someone."

"Terpsichore, if he gets close to you. Use your Muse powers."

"What Muse power exactly?"

"If you dance, the Goddesses and cosmic center will descend into you, and he won't cause you any harm."

"Dance? How can I dance when I am full of fear?"

"Trust your inner nature and the cosmos. It will be done."

The light and apparition faded. "Atropos. ATROPOS!" My knees buckled. "No, don't leave!"

I paced back and forth. 'What am I going to do? Dance? What kind of dance? Dancing will get me out of this? Dancing is the answer?"

A few days had passed when a guard entered with an elaborate saffron dress. He threw it at me. "Get ready and put this on. You're having dinner with the Magi."

I slipped into the dress a little tight, but it did not hinder my movements. The guard entered and led me to the Shadowbearded One's tent.

"Ahhh, much better," he said, sipping his wine and staring at my figure.

"Back to those questions. Where are you from?" He said softly.

"I...I am from the living Earth. She is my grandmother. And I am born from sacred waters." It was vague but accurate.

He swept his hand over neatly slicked-back hair, tapped his cup with his long manicured nails, raised it, and took a long drink.

He threw the cup across the room, lounged, and grabbed my wrist. "You will tell me your name. You will tell me your gift. I sense magic within you. I can smell it. I can feel it. And I can taste it." Seething, his wide eyes, and snarling mouth were waiting for my answer.

"Yes, I can tell you my gift, but it's best to show you. Since it does not use words."

He calmed and settled back a little, letting go of my wrist. Tilting away, he took another cup from the table and filled it with more wine. "Good, you are starting to listen."

He ordered the guard, "Leave and do not come in with another mishap, and don't come in no matter what you hear!" Dismissively shaking his hand.

With a cup of wine, he sat on the cushions and attentively waited.

Trembling and shaking, I shifted inward and centered my inner being. Was this going to work? What if the power doesn't come? She remembered Atropo's words, *trust*.

I thought back to one of the resilient trees I used to dance beneath at home—rooted, enduring. I steadied this Muse body, and my right foot edged forward. Pressing my toes into the earth, I turned swiftly, rotating around. My toes finished where they had begun, marking a circle around me on the ground. I let go and dropped into the body. From the top of my head, a great swoosh rushed and waved through me. Heat and lifeforce descended into my back to my sacrum and the ground below. My hips began to sway side to side, mesmerizing his gaze. As I raised my arms upward, light poured over me.

He bent closer.

My arms waved in a hypnotic pattern. My shoulders sauntered, turned, and released more and more with each breath. I raised my left foot and stomped it into the ground, inviting in a powerful surge that lit the entire tent. Overflowing through me, it filled the space. I felt a freedom and connection so great that it was as if I had merged with the whole cosmos. A brightness and ecstasy so immense that the world around me fell away.

"I heard a faint moan and cry. As the energy waned, I saw the Magi lying on his side, his eyes hollow and blind, his long-pointed, shadowbeard singed away. He couldn't withstand the light.

Dashing for the exit, I pulled back the tent flap. Guards and Magi were running and scattering in all directions. As beams of light flashed over the encampment. One man yelled, "Athena!" In golden armor with a flaming sword, she descended from the sky. The blade cut through the blue flame torches in one sharp swoop, breaking the spell. She ascended as swiftly as she arrived.

My sisters gathered me and set us miles away on a whirlwind. Dark clouds spun and twisted over the encampment, destroying and disintegrating whatever was left.

"Sister, are you ok? Did he hurt you?"

"No, I'm fine, sisters, but I feel tired. None of you told me about the ways of humans."

"We were all waiting for the right time. We are sorry, sister. Some yearn to keep the Muse and creative powers for themselves, to take advantage of or use in a controlling way. Power makes some of them drunk, and they decline instead of shine. Not all Magi, those humans who wield power, are like this. Most desire to benefit and heal the world. We must discern with a Muses' eye when meeting one. And who we are to inspire in a relationship," said Polyhymnia.

Urania hugged me close. "You're safe, let's go home."

Part III – The Gifted Thread

Months passed. In the spring, the Fates visited. Mother was overjoyed, and Erato was ecstatic. Though my spirit and vitality were restored, something still troubled me. I couldn't recall anyone ever speaking about dancing.

"Oh, no, we told you," Mother said. "But perhaps you were too young. Maybe you forgot. You must get this from your father." She threw her hands over her head. "Huh. I never thought I'd say *those* words in this house. You see, at birth, you were not yet ready to carry and dance the entire universe through your body. Your energy was powerful, and we did not want you to destroy the solar system. So the Fates suggested waiting until you were resilient enough to contain these frequencies, sweetie. That is one reason for their visit. It's a sort of right of passage."

Sometimes, Mother was so matter-of-fact about things. Maybe it was from having nine children. As for the memory itself, I am sure she was right. I could not recall ever dancing.

"That's because we helped you forget," said Atropos, sipping her tea and eyeing the double-chocolate lavender-berry cake. Lachesis smirked. "You can have a piece after dinner, sister."

"I already foresaw it, Lachesis!"

Atropos, the oldest and wisest of the ancients, tried to stand from her chair, her eyes hidden behind thick sunglasses. "Ophh, Earth is so dense! How do you all manage? Anyway, let's get to this…ahh, right of passage. Or whatever else you are calling it these days."

"Terpsichore, come forward, let me see you." She put her hands on my shoulders and pressed my arms, checking if my bones were ready for what was to come. "Gooood, good, good. Okay, we can proceed. Lachesis, fetch the toolbox, and please find Clothos!"

They brought back a large wooden box filled with weaving tools.

Atropos began. "Polyhymnia, if you are willing, sing a hymn of sleep for Terpsichore."

Polyhymnia signed the air with symbols, singing and chanting sweetly. I felt like I was falling into nothingness. Mother and my sisters held hands and watched the weavers work. Atropos unsealed an unseen gate above my head. Where the tendrils of energy flow into both gods and humans alike. First, Clothos returned the gifted string and removed the lesser replica running through my spine. Next, Lachesis took bunches of threads in an array of colors to support and fortify the new currents. Last, Atropos combed the threads in her wise hands and stretched them back to the Tree of Life. With a nod, Lachesis brought over a red box. A bright and delicate golden thread, a signature of the cosmic dance, laid on white fabric. With tweezers, Atropos carefully held the string and checked it over. Satisfied, she wove the thread from the lower sacred centers to the outer fringes of the cosmos.

At dusk, Polyhymnia's song called me home, and I opened my eyes. My body ached, and my legs found it challenging to step. I fell straight to the ground, and tingling spread through every bone, muscle, and cell.

"You might feel a little woozy for a few days as the activation recalibrates your system, Terpsichore. Integrating and learning how to dance differently will take time. You are the embodiment of the cosmic dance of life and of freedom," said Lachesis.

Atropos sat and dozed off with heavy eyelids. Lachesis walked by and said, "Cake, sister." Athropos jumped out of the chair and joined us as we made our way to celebrate in the dining hall.

"This is how I was gifted with dance. It took many years to learn the steps, how to let go and surrender to the universal flow, and who to inspire. I realized this is a way to channel Divine energy into this realm and live it, as is your birthright. All of life is a moment and a Divine dance unfolding."

Her tone turned cautionary. "Initiate, I also want to convey this: there may be predators, those who try to take your light. It is not always easy to discern who they are. I've had several encounters with such Beings and other stories yet to tell. But take heed: be diligent in protecting your gifts. As Muses, we expand and flourish them, but you must hold them close and honor them."

Terpsichore went to the banquet table and brought back two slices of cake. She laughed. "This is Atropos's favorite."

A Magical Vessel, Born of Gaea

Primal Being of the living Earth
You who are connected to the stars
Keeper of instinct, wisdom, and truth
Being of untamed wild nature,
vessel of the Divine

Embodiment of Goddess
Body, an offering of life
A gift from the ground
Merging humanity and mystery,
with gesture, posture, and movement

An Ancestor of sacred stories
through your bones
A transmission through time
Steps from their memory,
descending into life

The dance of each desire
Through gates of fire
An inner power grows
Extending into life,
for it's dance is freedom

Her Cosmic Waltz

1 Inspired, she dances as a flame.
2 With emotion, she flows and bends like a great river.
3 Aspecting power, her body carries the voice of the Earth.

1 The wild one with hair flying around fires in a rhythmic nature.
2 A tempest storm of downpours and twisting cycles of changes.
3 The storyteller, who moves from the power in her bones.

1 The heat and passion of an intimate dance.
2 The fluidity of holding hands in a circle, scribing songs into the ground.
3 The stepping in unison, in rows, stomping spells into stones.

Beyond mind in pure movement
Beyond time in total union
Surrendering to this cosmic dance

Journey of Dance & Embodiment

"Prepare Initiate for this journey of dance," Terpsichore said.

Get into aomfortable position and begin to notice your body. Breathe deeply in and out a few times. Breathe even further into your body, letting out a sound. Continue to focus on your breath. Relax and let go of any tension. Expand into your body and feel its edges. Bring your attention to your feet. Sense the powerful force of Nature and the living Earth beneath you. Draw its life-giving energy up through your feet and allow it to flow through your body.

Feel warmth spread into your ankles, moving up to your calves and knees. Let this revitalizing heat move through your thighs, buttocks, lower back, and abdomen up to your chest. Relax as the energy moves into your shoulders, arms, and hands. The inviting warmth continues, soothing your throat and flowing up to your forehead and to the top of your crown. Breathe. See the warm, radiant light moving out from the top of your head, connecting to the cosmic star above. Sense, hear, see this vibration simmering all around you, shining in all directions, expanding you.

As you expand further out, notice rays of vibrant light approaching you, dancing and glittering exquisitely. Colors you have yet to experience draw near. A beam of light stretches toward you, gently gathering you and whisking you above the land. Below are people, animals, plants, rivers, and tides ebbing and flowing.

Traveling through the sky, between clouds, you spot an ancient stone temple below. The vibrant light lowers you to the ground. In front of you, a path illuminated by fire-clay vessels leads you to the top of the steps. The temple is silhouetted against the rising full moon, and the faint scent of incense carries on the breeze. In the distance, you hear the rhythmic pulse of a drum.

From the top of the step, approach the open space and notice the stone temple ground, with fire and flame dancing at its center. Behind the blaze, several women in orange and red robes move to the rhythm of the drums. The fire grows brighter, sparks flying into the evening sky. One woman extends her hand, and you join her. Immerse yourself in the liveliness as she leads you around the flames, twirling, spinning, and gliding with ease. Feel the sensations rising within you. (Pause)

The drumbeats deepen and intensify. Several Priestesses enter, carrying censers with burning red coals. They begin to spin, and smoke billows into the atmosphere. The great fire at the center grows twice its size. (Pause)

The drums' rhythms increase as another woman gracefully enters from behind the fire and smoke. A scent of sweet jasmine and herbs surrounds her. You watch as she undoes her hair, letting it cascade over her shoulders. She offers her hand to you and leads you in a dance. As she spins you, many join in, raising the power of the sacred space.

"You see and feel everything around the temple in motion, a dynamic expression of life. As you return your gaze to her, the cosmos shine in her eyes. She continues to guide you in this ecstatic embrace. She has a message for you, something you have been waiting to hear for a long time. Take time to listen and ask her questions. (Pause)

The music begins to slow, and people start to disperse. The Priestess leads you to a set of ancient double doors at the side of the temple. A creative gift resides beyond these doors. Use your key to locate the gift and bring it back. (Pause)

It's time to finish up and make your way back. At the temple, the central fire burns low, and the first light of dawn breaks through the clouds to the east. Though it is time to leave, know that you can return to this place whenever you wish. The Priestess leads you to the entryway. Ask her any final questions you may have, and then offer her a gesture of gratitude for the journey. (Pause)

Make your way back toward the path and the flaming vessels. Ahead, you see the vibrant light that guided you. Step in and let the light return you across the land to your room. Thank the light and come back to your body.

Terpsichore's Well-Wish

"Rest in your body and ground your feet as I send you off with a set of well-wishes."

Let me gift you these creative shoes
so you may dance past limitations, disappointments, and despair
when things become dark, draining, or overwhelming.

So you may dance with trust in the movement
of your creative self
and step into life and live it fully.

So you may dance the ways of your truth
and break free from the things
that don't let you stretch.

So you may dance with the joys
and learn to step past the sorrows
when things become too heavy.

So you may dance upon shooting stars
extend into grace, and into the arms of love.

May I have this dance?
The one where we lead each other
holding hands, filled with love.

My well-wishes to you, dancer, and your feet
for all the steps you will take in life,
Terpsichore

J. WELLS KARA

Chapter X
Thalia: Muse of Comedy

"Laughter is the shortest distance between two people." —Plato

I CALLED OUT AS I CONTINUED DOWN THE CORRIDOR. "ELLA, ELLA!"."Yes, yes, don't worry!" The Wayfinder said, properly adjusting her hat. "I'm fine, Grace. How did it go with Terpsichore? I see you found the door."

"Her story is an important lesson."

"She is powerful, and yes, the Muses are not to be taken lightly." Ella adjusted her robe and sleeves. "Now, we're off to the youngest of the Muses, Thalia. We'll be taking a different path."

"I hoped you'd share some of your adventures."

"Hmmm, some other time. We have places to be." Ella walked briskly ahead. "Keep pace, Initiate."

I barely matched her stride, and as I turned the corner, she appeared upside down on the ceiling.

"What the hell, Ella?!"

"Initiate, take a step, you'll make this way with ease."

Placing a foot forward, my whole perspective shifted. I was traveling right-side up, or up-side-down, or perhaps in some other direction entirely. My stomach dropped into my throat, my hair stood on end, and my keys dangled wildly from my pocket.

"That's Thalia for you." Ella chuckled.

We approached a door with a box inside the threshold. Inside the box are riddles, quotes, and flashing lights.

The sign read:

"To gain entry, you must tell a joke."

Ella put her hand over her mouth. "Try to play along."

How had I gotten myself into this? I reminded myself this was the realm of the Muse, where nothing was predictable.

"Here's one I remember: What did the ocean say to the beach? Nothing. It just waved."

The box lights strobed, clicked, and rattled. From the bottom sprang a yellow note:

"Tell one more for the door."

Ella reached into her pockets. "Yeah, that one didn't quite land. Try again."

"What did the stars say to the moon? Wow, you've really changed!" A mechanism clicked, and the box slid open.

"You got her attention," said Ella. "I'll wait for you."

Venturing inside, I tripped across the entrance and stumbled, landing in the middle of a party on top of a jester wearing a large purple bow tie.

"Happy birthday!" Thalia exclaimed with sweet laughter, throwing paper confetti all around me. The troupe joined in, blowing party favors and merrily singing.

"My birthday was months ago, Thalia."

"Every day is your birthday. You are born each day, each moment, and every second. You are alive! Creating, making, building, birthing. You know."

Thalia continued her prancing, poking her face into mine. "You haven't been celebrating your existence, have you?"

I chuckled, touched by a wave of giddy energy that fluttered inside me. Uncontrollable joy bubbled up in my body and mind, overwhelming me with a transcendent lightness.

"Yes, feel it rise in you, the uncontrollable laughter of life, the sigh of amusement, the smiles of delight. The glimpses of glee, the splendor of joy. In the realm of the absurd, where normal rules don't apply to predictable physics.

You break free from a box that never existed. You are swept into laughter, realizing the illusion."

She lifted a glass of bubble water and fruit.

"I celebrate you
I celebrate me,
We laugh together
On this journey!"

She gave me the Fool card. "Are you ready to be vulnerable? To reinvigorate your soul with humor and jest? Yes?"

"Open to the ways of the mask of comedy and its medicine," she continued. "It's saturated with satire, banter, and play. The one who wears the joyful mask breaks through hard truths. It releases the rigid, the serious, the outdated. This mask helps society leap through fears, tribulations, and all the indoctrination that has shaped it. When laughter is present, judgment is absent. The mind shuts off the suffering ego and spins unexpected beginnings and endings. The trickster wears the mask to challenge beliefs, limitations, and the pedantic. Their last laugh bridges life, moving forward in a new way together.

The humor of creation, the feast of life. Let the mask of comedy loosen your grip and relieve the pressure of resistance. Where you find laughter, burdens ease.

Clear the path to your younger self, to the excitement of play. I bring the lightness to the mundane. I shift your perspective through twists and turns. Behind and upside down, I am the Divine Fool, stepping into the new."

A Joyful Destiny

I gazed at Thalia's mask. "Yes, Initiate, let me share the story of how I became the Muse of Comedy."

Part I – The Art of Laughter

Many summers before the endless days of rain, in the early tides of Greece, lived an old magical woodcarver. He and his wife were masters at their arts and crafts. They made dazzling pouring vessels, flutes, cups, carts, and boats. All the neighbors purchased their wares; some were prized and sold miles away by merchants. The entire community adored the couple. Each evening, the old woodcarvers would visit different homes, sharing stories, laughter, and tales that brought everyone together.

Late one night, as the old woodcarver worked on his latest creation, three coals fell out of the fire to the floor. Unbeknownst to him, one of the coals ignited a wooden staff ablaze. Within minutes, the embers spread, consuming the room and walls, and flames engulfed the entire house. Trapped, the woodcarver shouted for his wife, but by morning, all that remained were charred timbers and ashes and wisps of smoke in a darkened sky. The woodcarver and his wife had vanished without a trace.

When the community heard the heavy news, it dampened their hearts and even saddened the cows that grazed on their land. How could such a tragedy occur?

By evening, everyone gathered at the shoreline and adorned one of the woodcarver's boats with fabric, shells, and a straw representation of the couple. Over the bow, a lantern to guide them to the other world. Some placed trinkets, dolls, stones, and cakes by their feet as tokens of gratitude and to honor their passage. Others wept, and some stood frozen with despair.

The community tried to get back to some resemblance of normalcy. But the grief went on for months, and winter came early. They had closed their doors, locked their windows, and stocked their food. They forgot to celebrate the sun's return, and the neighbors didn't check on each other.

Several weeks into spring, a strange sight suffused the sky. The entire night flared with streams of greens, purples, and pinks. The event had caused people to trickle out of their homes and to the shore. After three days, the light dimmed. People retreated home until one of the neighbors spotted an object on the beach. He darted over and washed off the sand.

It was a joyful wooden mask.

"Hey, look!" the man called out, breathless. "It's from the old woodcarver, a gift from beyond!"

The community gathered in awe. One by one, smiles returned.

Part II – Truth in the Mask

The whole community gathered and agreed to take turns caring for the mask. This is where the story shifts into the realm of the creative spirit.

One of the elders hung the mask high on the wall for safekeeping and instructed the household to watch over it with great care. But his tall, older grandson, who knew better, had taken an interest in the mask. One day, when his grandfather and the other villagers left early to fish, the grandson tiptoed into the main room. He reached out his long arms and took the mask from the wall. Without a thought, he placed it over his face.

At first, nothing happened, but then the mask began to grow in power, altering and shaping him. He tried to remove it, but it wouldn't budge, no matter how hard he pulled and wrenched. Panicking, he bolted from the house, running toward the village and screaming for help.

One of the neighbors recognized the grandson and stopped him. "What's wrong?" the man asked.

Brashly, the grandson jumped forward. "I am the truth-teller! Nothing is wrong with your leg; you limp to avoid work!" The man quickly glanced around, hoping no one had heard, then grabbed the boy and whispered, "Who told you?"

Seeing the man's distress, the grandson took off and ran to where a crowd had started to form. He began to tell jokes about everyone in town. Neighbors laughed at neighbors until the laughter turned on them. Truth upon truth, until everyone started laughing in uncontrollable fits. For days, the village laughed, drunk with stupor and frenzy, forgetting all their troubles but also forgetting to feed their horses, milk the cows, and open their shops.

Unable to remove the mask, the grandson watched in horror as the village descended into chaos. Determined to make things right, he fled, running far from the town to save them from the havoc he had caused. He headed for the high hills, hoping to find someone to help; he ran farther and farther upward until lost and exhausted. Parched, he knelt by a spring, drank its waters, and fell into a dream-woven sleep.

Part III – The Fill of Joy

And that is where I found him, by one of our enchanted wells, curled up, asleep for days. The young boy was too inexperienced to handle the power of the mask and not aware of comedic timing. I carefully loosened it from his face and set it aside. What was I to do with such an object? Just then, Mother and Lachesis arrived.

"It looks like the mask has found its rightful owner," said Lachesis.

"The boy?" I exclaimed.

"Thalia, the mask belongs to you," said Mother, throwing up her hands. "You are the Muse of Comedy and Reprieve, it's already been foretold. Haven't you noticed that you've been telling jokes and pranking your sisters since you first came into this world?"

Lachesis held the mask. "The old woodcarver and his wife were much older than most believed. These master-makers were divinely gifted, but they didn't comprehend the amount of magic imbued in their objects. We are fortunate the mask is not in the possession of a relic collector. Thalia, you are destined to learn the ways of the mask and inspire the comedic spirit in humans."

"And what if I say no? Don't I get a choice in the matter?" Thalia pouted and crossed her arms.

"Thalia, some things are fated." Mneme glanced at Lachesis. "Sorry."

"Can't Klio or Calliope do this? Why me? What would happen if I didn't accept the mask?"

Lachesis took Thalia's hand and looked inward, glimpsing further into the future. "Then the entire human collective would be without a powerful way to process suffering, fear, burdens, rigidity, and disaster. Some parts of human life would wither without the sun of joy. Without laughter to shake them awake."

Thalia felt the weight of the world's suffering at that moment. "Ok, ok, ok, I get it! You didn't have to go full doom and gloom on me!"

"Thalia, what is the one thing you wish for mortals?" Mother asked.

"For everyone to get along, move past barriers, and be happy!" Thalia responded.

"You see, your gift is already who you are, Thalia," Lachesis said, offering the mask to her.

Thalia took the mask in her hands. "I'm not going to argue with Fate, but what if I don't like it?"

"Maybe try it part-time, sweetie. See how it feels. The mask is meant to be put on and taken off."

Mother had a valid point.

I wasn't sure at first, but then I slipped on the mask. Instantly, each part of me expanded with a buzz of pure joy. Uncontrollable laughter rippled across the cosmos. Swept up in the mirth, mortals, gods, and goddesses smiled. Even the most solemn souls couldn't help but chuckle. The laughter wiped away sadness, anger, and fear from the world—for a brief spell. Can you imagine if it had lasted five whole minutes?

"My work began at that moment. My first task was to reunite the boy with his family and help the village recover from a week of continuous laughter. Despite sore muscles and back pain from being doubled over, everyone survived. As for the boy, he became a gifted musician known for his antics across many lands. One of his descendants would go on to become a renowned and spirited comedian."

I've told you how I became the keeper of the mask. Yes, I was reluctant at first, yet my excitement and sense of purpose grew. Still, the journey wasn't easy; the mask was only beginning to reveal its truth..."

Thaliophóros

Laughter is freedom if you can see
bridging the distance between you and me
returning to the present, a mind in freefall
no thinking, no judgment, no worry at all

A carefree journey into the unknown
carrying paradox and discovery alone
catching with words of what not to say
with absurdity and mirth and play

Lighthearted banter and joyful tales
satire, farce, and witty fails
liveliness and jesting comedy
reflecting all of life as a parody

Journey with the Joyful Mask

"Allow me to take you on a journey to visit your joy," Thalia said, settling herself. *"Initiate, sit, or lay down in a comfortable position."*

Notice your body and breathe deeply in and out a few times. Breathe further into your body, belly, and chest. Slowly, let out an aaaahhh sound a few times, expanding the heart's energy. Continue to sink further into the chair or the floor below you, lengthening your breath out.

Begin to see a door. Notice the color, texture, smell, and style. Are there any symbols on this door? Now, turn the handle and go through.

As you cross the threshold, you notice a procession moving toward you, headed for a nearby village. Notice the atmosphere of where you are. Is it a country or place you can identify? Is it an ancient site or a future one to come? Sense the air, smell the colors, and feel the temperature. As the procession nears you, sounds of music, joy, and laughter grow brighter and fuller.

A few members wave to you to join in; some are flying flags, playing drums, and singing. Some jesters don the mask of comedy. A few juggle, some mime, and others are telling jokes.

You feel a tap on your shoulder, and you turn; a charismatic Priestess is wearing a joyful mask. She briefly lifts the mask, offering you a playful smile before extending her hand. As you take it, she dashes into the crowd. You follow, moving and twirling until you reach the village. She gestures, does a few flips, and runs to a door that is off to the side. This door takes you back to one of the most joyous moments in your life when you were fully present and in the moment. Use your creative key to unlock the door and go through. Be open to what you experience. (Pause)

Begin to make your way back from the event and through the door to the Priestess. Ask her any questions you might have about what you encountered.

Why did this event present itself to you? Notice how it felt and who you were with, if anyone. (Pause)

As she finishes, the Priestess leads you to another door. This passage is to a place where you've forgotten, hidden, or rejected a part of your playful self. Take your key, unlock the door, and go inside. Find this missing part of yourself and let it know it is safe to return back to you. (Pause)

Start to finish up and begin to make your way back to the Priestess. As you exit, she takes your hand, and together, you spin clockwise into a room with a mirror. In your hand is your mask of comedy; hold it to your face and take note of its details and the materials it's made from. Now, invite that lost, playful side of yourself to rejoin your life. Assure this part of yourself that you are able to keep them safe. Call them back into your life with open arms. Ask what they need from you to make the integration easier. (Pause)

With a magical gesture, the Priestess summons a wand. She zips and zags it over your head to help this part of you to reintegrate into life. After, you both return to the group, which is dancing and playing music.

The Priestess leads you to the edge of the village, telling you to come back whenever you wish. She shares a few words of inspiration and wisdom about laughter and comedy. (Pause)

When she's finished, offer her a token of gratitude. Then, retrace the procession's path, returning to where you began, moving back into your body and into the room.

Thalia's Well-Wish & a Riddle

"Before you go, let me happily share this well-wish and riddle with you.

When things are demanding and despair is near
When things become confusing and unclear

When you are lost and completely lose sight
When the world is absent or doesn't feel right

When obstacles and challenges block your way
When your heartaches for love to stay

Then, take a great leap from the ground
Look another way, turn upside-down
Spin in a circle and lift your frown

Continue to skip along your path,
with a grin, a chuckle, and many laughs.

—Who begins, ends, and begins again,
 never touching the ground, yet stands upon a peak?

With loving hugs,
Thalia

Chapter XI

Calliope: Muse of Epic Poetry
& Storytelling

"In every hero's story, the Gods and Goddesses play their part, for no fate is ever free from their hand." —Hesiod (adapted)

STUMBLING OUT OF THE DOORWAY. I lost my balance. "I've got you," said Ella. "Am I right side up or the other way down?" I struggled to stand and find my feet.

She took my hand. "You will when we take the next right. Keep hold of me."

Bracing myself and clasping tight, I let her guide me through the corridor as we made the smooth transitional shift.

"Ah, a little perspective change is wholesome for the soul," she said, readjusting her robe.

"We are on the way to visit Calliope, the oldest of the Muses. Put on these rain boots. We will be navigating through several waterways ahead." Ella warned.

I didn't ask or try to interpret what she meant but simply sat and shimmied on the knee-high boots. "Okay, I'm ready."

And there were many deep springs, gusty winds, and heavy downpours. The Hall rocked like a ship in a hurricane. Hailstones the size of pebbles pelted the walls, adding to the chaos. The path was unclear, and the lines between the walls blurred. I could not discern where some things ended and others began.

Ahead, Ella walked on like nothing was amiss, as if the sun was shining. "You're doing great," she said, not even checking if I was still alive.

"This was not in the brochure, Ella. You need to send someone out to make repairs. And you're right. I am questioning all my life choices."

Ella laughed.

The fierce elements softened as she stopped in front of an ancient wooden door. The thick frame was secured with gold hinges and an odd-shaped bright crystal handle.

Soaked, cold, and pissed off, I wrung out my drenched hair and wiped my face.

Ella stood at the door, clearly holding back from commenting. "This is the threshold to Calliope."

Without sparing her a glance, I knocked once, rotated the handle, and walked through the door. My wet shoes sloshed with every step, leaving a trail of water in my wake.

Ella began her usual, "I'll be waiting…" but I shut the door before she could finish.

She could have at least offered a raincoat.

I was in a wooden room with the scent of aged timber and the faint crackle of fire. In the corner, a massive hearth roared, flickering shadows above lanterns glowing like distant stars. The shelves were crammed with books and delicate glass terrariums, little ecosystems of forgotten worlds. I was aboard a ship, but what was its destination?

I stood in front of the fire to dry my hair and clothes. Over the mantelpiece hung a striking relief of nine women, each with their instruments and wreaths, dancing in a harmonious celebration. Their presence gazed onward like guardians of the arts and Mysteries.

"Hello, Initiate! I see you made it through the gauntlet," Calliope said.

"Yeah, about that…"

Calliope picked up a long pipe and, with a snap of her fingers, set its contents flaming. Smoke drifted and curled into the air.

"Is smoking wise?"

"It's dried apples and flowers. Think of it as aromatherapy. It's harmless. Come on, let's sit by the fire," Calliope said.

She took a few puffs and pulled out her pen and book. Curious, she sensed me. The room fell into a comfortable and expansive silence.

Like all Muses, she radiated an otherworldly beauty. Her long, dark brown curls were casually gathered into a messy bun. A crown of jewels rested atop her head. She wore a long green gown embroidered with exquisite patterns. Her form was graceful, with hands that have carried and completed countless stories, millions of pages scribed over thousands of years. When she spoke, her voice was a melody of dreams. It could enliven and inspire any tired heart. I could have listened to her evocative, timeless words for eternity.

I sat close to the fire, not sure whether I felt more alive or undone. Calliope watched me as if she knew every answer I hadn't thought to ask.

"Let me share with you the tale of the Muse and her stories, dear Initiate."

Quiet and wide-eyed, I listened as if her voice had called something ancient in me awake.

"As Muse and Storyteller, I ride with you on this incredible journey. In a place where the tides of emotion and eloquent words embrace each other. They flow across the living waters, moving through you, weaving the tales yet to be told. Those who invoke me and channel me bring a spark of inspiration that transcends the mundane.

Many called upon my name to breathe life into their story, but few heeded the wisdom I offered. There is a sacred path to stories, myths, and the ageless truths they hold. You must find out why you write your stories. Why do you weave and craft certain tales? Who is the One telling the story? What do you learn from the characters in your life? Are they not as true as any embodied friend? What you create impacts all, as art leaves its lasting mark.

We are all timeless myths embarking on an epic journey of aliveness. We are woven from the countless stories of love but also from the influences of conditioning. Each step is an unfolding chapter of discovery. The grand adventure across oceans, upon other worlds, or through great distances of time may seem epic and a fantastic tale. Yet the most epic journey and the most incredible story is awakening to who you are. Whether you realize it or not, that is part of why you're writing, yes?

Those who live the path of storytellers craft tales that guide, warn, and inspire. They are the keepers of vision, the seers who peer past the rumble of destruction beyond the fleeting present and into rebirth. Your stories are not mere words but catalysts for awakening. They breathe life into all who listen.

Stories shape us and offer a mirror to our souls. When the world suffers loss or fragmentation, we need stories more than ever. When you write, you invite clarity, wisdom, and healing. Each word you pen uncovers truths hidden deep within you and within the collective. Through your stories, you reconnect not only with yourself but across time.

We are the most remarkable stories of humanity. Those who rise above unimaginable challenges, forge paths through darkness and doubt, and endure relentless adversity prove that the impossible can be transcended. What was once unreachable becomes within our grasp and the collective's. We are beacons, lighting the way for the world.

We are the emerging stories and possibilities manifesting the things to come. The myths that will forever change the landscape. Each soul waiting to speak itself into the world. Within you, a living spark, a poem, capable of changing destinies and crafting a brighter, limitless future.

Take care of this spark and feed its fire. For your words are endless possibilities with the power to shape a world."

Calliope's Journey Home

"Let us journey into how I became the Muse of Epic Poetry and Storytelling. Would you mind grabbing a few logs from the corner and putting them on the fire? We have some long hours ahead," Calliope said, lighting a candle.

Part I – The Call of the Sea

As the firstborn, by an hour and a day, I had much of the responsibility of caring for my younger siblings. Each sister had her own temperament, sensitivity, and gift, which trained me well in the art of diplomacy. My earliest memories are of constant movement, following our mother from one house to another. The endless upheaval and long journeys wore on us, leaving us weary. Ceaseless travel through uncertain lands.

I found solace in the realm of visions. To lift our spirits, I conjured grand sagas of charming Goddesses and mortal heroes, tales of fierce battles and fated love, impossible quests, and magical relics that could save the world.

But that is not where this story begins.

We begin on the high seas, aboard a weathered ship in a great storm. When humans followed the stars, intuited the water, and smelled the rain. A time when the oldest storytellers emerged from the dream world and imagination. When consciousness started to recognize itself.

This is where we began, under the floorboards in a small room far out at sea, with an audacious captain with a penchant for trouble. Consider him a pirate in this story. He was proud, vivacious, and passionate and enjoyed dancing and yelling from the deck, especially in storms with sizable waves. He was forever scheming to outwit the Fates. I would have thought him a God if he didn't bleed so easily.

If you're squinting at these words, thinking I was the captive—I was not. But fate had other plans, steering me toward my destiny.

A month earlier, Mneme continued her persistent attempts to marry me off to a lesser god. She never forced any of my sisters into this nonsense, so it was either a wedding or set sail. I picked the latter, making my swift exit. Mother hoped at least one of us would give her grandchildren. Maybe she assumed it was my responsibility as the eldest.

Suitor after suitor, of all shapes, creatures, and sizes, visited. I half considered the octopus because, you know, he's so quiet and an excellent multi-tasker. This had gone on for years. At our last meeting, I'd had enough.

"This ends now. My decision is final. I won't marry anyone until I'm ready!" I said.

"You are in those books and the imaginative realm too much, Calliope. I hoped you would get out in the world and meet someone."

"Mother, I sense your concern, but this isn't the time!"

But still, the suitors came, so I packed my things and left without a word to my sisters. I intended to seek out Artemis and Aunt Aoede, and a visit to the Fates was long overdue. Besides, I couldn't shake the feeling of a calling and longing within me.

A few villages over, I stopped at a full tavern and asked the innkeeper who commanded the seas best. Without hesitation, he pointed to a gentleman, or in this case, the pirate of this story.

His large, attractive eyes were pierced with life. A mustache and trimmed dark beard outlined his full ruby lips. Draped in a long, fine cloak with tattered fringes, one hand gracefully rested on his hip, the other cradled a cup of wine. I watched him closely, listening to his tales and playful banter. He had that bard-like spirit, charming, sharp-witted, and undeniably striking. But you could tell he had fallen overboard one too many times. And beneath it all, he was running, but from whom, or what?

I approached him. His eyes widened, and he caught himself.

"They say you navigate the seas like the Gods."

"But of course, my Lady! I've learned a few tricks from them." He started to stand and bow. "My name is Andrea. And you are?"

"Calliope, I am searching for Artemis. Have you heard of her in the Western Isles?"

"The Goddess of the Wild. Yes. That was her last sighting, and that region is home to many temples dedicated to her. It's the first place I would look, fine Lady." His grin was broad.

I knew this type, someone chasing their next adventure. "What is your price?"

"Four silver bags, nothing less." Was his quick response.

"And the duration?"

He moved his hands as if working through an invisible equation. Studying the stars, he calculated. "Three weeks."

"And so it is." I agreed.

Within a few days, he had rustled together a crew, several barrels of wine, and a dog for the journey west. With things in order, we set sail on smooth waters, for the moment at least.

Part II – A Storyteller's Dream

"Good Lady, what's so urgent in the Western Isles with Artemis that has you in such haste?"

"Like you, I desire an adventure. I have not seen Artemis in many years and seek her wisdom." *And she also holds a possession of mine that I need to reclaim.*

We watched as the distant, dark clouds of a heavy storm brewed.

He gave caution while extending his head past the bow. "Let's hope Poseidon is in our favor, Lady. The way the clouds are mounting, Zeus must be upset with us mortals. The worst of it will pass, but the waves will give this weathered ship a ride and tussle. Might be wise to go below and secure your things."

Descending below deck, I made my way past hundreds of vessels filled with wine and spices. I saw why he was concerned.

I settled into the cozy, quaint cabin overflowing with elegant rugs, fine pottery, and ancient siren reliefs; the pirate had an eye for art and finery. Tossing a few branches into the short stove, I murmured an incantation under my breath. Flames sprang to life, igniting both the hearth and the nearby oil lamps. Then came the soft chair, which I sank into for a demanding rest and drifted, my inner vision opening.

My sight settled me under a vast, star-strewn sky. Five Ancient Ones, women, sat in a circle around a dancing fire. Their faces were lined with time. They were not the Fates, yet they felt just as powerful. I watched in silence the rhythmic pull of their needles across the cloth. Each one stitched a different pattern with a deliberate, unseen purpose. Their mouths moved in unison with sounds of ancient syllables beyond language.

Waayheee, Waayheee, Waayheee
Onnnanana, Onnnanana, Onnnanana
Maazarrrrinnn, Maazarrrrinnn, Maazarrrrinnn
Borrashhia, Borrashhia, Borrashhia
Shoowhoshhhh, Shoowhoshhhh, Shoowhoshhhh

Each sound poured from them, a chant into the fabric of life. One of them spoke and pointed to a stone in the circle. "Sit, young Muse."

"We are the Storytellers." They said in unison, continuing their work.

What realm did they belong to, mortal or Divine?

"Yes." They all said.

"Calliope, we have been calling you. Why have you not answered?"

I attuned inward, and a flood of memories poured over me. Recurring dreams from my childhood show me the future, this moment.

"Why did you call me in my youth? What is this destiny?"

"You have not answered." One spoke, glaring at me with a single eye while the other watched the stitching.

"Muse, we have been calling you to set your gift into motion." Said the eldest. Her dark skin glowed, her silver curls forming a starry crown, and her eyes shimmered with nurturing and love.

"I gather this has to do with storytelling."

"Yes, you learn quickly." She replied.

"There are new stories to be told and heroes to unfold. There is much healing to be done and poems to be sung. There are epic tales to tell and wonders to unveil." Chuckled the one with the large hat and toothy grin, who sang and stomped her feet.

"Your mother and her sister, Aoede, once sat in this circle, and the gift they carried has now passed to you. We are the ones who will guide you in the art of storytelling. To inspire those yet to come. You will learn to shape it in your own way," said the starry-eyed one.

I would not have accepted…but I knew that feeling, that unmistakable and forceful nudge from within. And there were the dreams, already written. "What is it that I need to do?"

"Sit, relax, and let the words and activation flow through you. This will last for a time and then conclude. Seek us when you need guidance; you will find us in the realm of dreams," one said.

The Five Ancient Ones exhaled in united breath to fuel the flames, coaxing them higher. As they began to sing, their voices carried an ancient story with forgotten wisdom. Energy swirled around us, spiraled, and danced in the night. It twirled faster with life and magic. My senses calmed, and my mind sank, still and quiet like a lake. A few stood in unison, raised their hands, and lifted their voices across time to a future song. Above me, the stars stirred, casting down radiant drops of stories yet to be told. They flickered like jewels around us. The pace quickened as the starry-eyed one conducted and directed the invocation. The magic gathered with momentum, and the elders clasped hands. Channeling the surging energy toward the crown of my head. It spiraled downward like a luminous vortex, merging inside me. A radiant current activated and sibilated through the fiber of my body.

I fell to the ground, tired and zapped. Traces of light hissed through my limbs. Beyond the fire, the Five Ancient Ones wove their song into the fabric of time, their needles guiding the cloth with stories. Hours slipped by, and then one stirred me from the depths. Her voice was soft yet resonant: "This part of the story is finished, Muse. You need to wake up."

I awoke to a cabin in complete turmoil. Books flew from the shelves. My chest flipped over onto the floor. The desk shuffled from one side to the other. My shoes tumbled. Papers flew, and ink spilled onto the floorboards. Hoping out of the chair, I secured my things with a rope and snuffed out the oil lamps.

On the other side of the door, crashing pottery, creaking planks, and churning water. The pirate yelled, half drunk, to his men to hurry with straw and netting. Scurrying from the upper and lower decks into the long hours of the night.

By morning, the tumultuous waves had subsided.

I unlatched the door and stepped onto a floor marked with oil, fruit, and wine stains. In the corner, the pirate lay shirtless, arms draped around his fellow seafarer. A full cup of wine still miraculously upright in his grasp. Navigating the scattered remnants, I crept over the mess and went above deck.

The saltwater smelled fresh as the sun reflected off the tranquil water. My mind drifted back to Five Ancient Ones. What did I set in motion? How does Artemis and Aoede fit into this unfolding tale?

The pirate blinked, trying to acclimate his eyes to the light while pulling his cloak tighter, then staggered over to me.

"Good, lady, how did you fair?"

"Fine, but the waves sounded on top of us."

"Your observations are correct. I had to order the crew to go below. But I knew this ship would hold steady, even if the cargo didn't. Waves like that are rare and unseasonal. I believe something was conjured. The sky and water are not in good spirits." He crossed his arms closer around himself. "We have less than a week. Let's hope Artemis will greet our arrival."

"He was right; something was conjured. But by whom? And for what purpose?"

"You are a talented captain, Andrea. No one else could have steered us through those surges."

Surprised, he nodded with pride and parted below deck.

Part III – The Wounds That Hunt Us

Finding my way topside, I found Andrea holding the dog.

"Ge, Ge!" His eyes sparkled. "Skylos can sense when we are close to land! Haha! His accuracy challenges the birds and the tides, especially after a storm!"

Excited to make landfall, the crew cleared the decks, lowered the sails, and maneuvered the rudder for docking. From the bow, the land stretched out in a vibrant shade of emerald. Trees packed so densely that not a patch of earth showed between them. The water is a striking cyan, in contrast to the deep greens of the forest. To the starboard side, a bustling plaza of merchants with distant voices chirping in the salty air. As we made land, I felt the magic afoot. The aether had that unworldly stillness and timeless background, indicating enchantment. Artemis must be around. "How long will you be docked?"

He put his finger in his mouth, held it to the wind, then turned to the sun and tides. At least until Boedromion when the Greater Mysteries commence in Athens. We're not invited, but that doesn't stop us from slipping into the procession every year." He grinned.

"Two months should be plenty of time," I told him.

"It will cost the Lady five silver bags to get back across. You paid one way."
"Why five?"

"For the extra cargo, you will stow. I'm certain you didn't journey all this way just to speak with a Goddess. Meet me in the plaza in a month to sort the arrangements." He waved and pivoted on his heels to a corner establishment.

Perhaps he was a God.

Leaving most of my belongings aboard the ship, I gathered the essential provisions and ventured to the densest forest. By a sacred spring, I made camp, kindled a fire, and traced the shape of a deer and moon into the soil. I hummed a chant taught to me by Polyhynmia. The shimmering symbol lifted, fluttered, and flew into the forest. Artemis will know it is me.

For five days, she did not appear. I changed my plans and resolved to wait until the seventh morning to leave. She might not be in the Western Isles, or she might not want to speak. The thought unsettled me.

Deep in the night, in slumber, I was awakened by a presence at my feet. Startled by a bright, silvery figure with a bow and arrow poised in still grace. "Artemis, you've come!

"Yes, Calliope. Quick, let's make our way to protected ground."

Artemis helped me pack my things. She easily tucked two large bags under each arm.

"Why did you bring so much with you?"

"These are my essentials."

"Huff." Artemis shook her head and made her way.

We ascended the island's mountain through a hidden cave and ancient pathway to one of her oldest temples. "This is my favorite temple. It has the best views," she said.

She put more wood on the fire and lit the temple candles. "Why have you come, Muse? I haven't seen you in many lunar months."

From her tone, she was displeased. "Artemis, I've come seeking your wisdom and Aoede's musical locket, which you have in your possession."

"I see. You disappeared before I could return it. I assumed you fled home. I heard you were accepting suitors?"

"Oh, no, no, no. Mother wanted me to marry, but I refused and left. Finding a sacred masculine counterpart is near impossible. Zeus is not setting a good example."

Artemis lifted an eyebrow. "So you come to me? Calliope, what Muse do you want?"

"What in Hades! Why is everyone asking me that!"

"Please don't announce his name. Calliope, you don't have to marry, but you can't go on avoiding these topics or your relationships. Besides, it is not helping your Muse energy."

"You are not married! You're free-spirited and charming, can shoot arrows thousands of miles across the sky, magically talk to animals, and go anywhere you please, within reason." I said, flustered.

"Calliope, I sense a wound within you. If you'll allow me, I can help you heal what's keeping you bound."

At my wit's end, I nodded and started pacing.

Artemis went to the table and chopped some roots and flowers. She finished with a sprinkle of moon water, making a concoction of tea. "Come sit by the fire, Calliope."

As I settled, she placed the hot cup of tea in my hand. "This may feel uncomfortable for a moment, but stay present with whatever arises. I will be right here beside you. When you're ready, ask, why does this wound exist?"

Calming myself, I sipped the bitter brew and watched the flames. They reminded me of the Five Ancient Ones and their songs until I noticed a shift. My hearing wavered, and my sight blurred. The walls pulsed in and out. I focused on the question: Why do I have this wound? The temple shook, faded, and dissolved.

A familiar scene opened in front of me. The cries of a newborn echoed as my mother came into view. Every unprocessed emotion washed over me and hers as well. The feelings of grief and aching loss.

Across the room, standing with command and authority, was my father, Zeus. "Mneme, don't be this way! I have the greater world to run and am bound to my duty. I am always on call!"

"Why can't you change things?" Mother said, tears streaming. "I love you, Zeus!"

He met her eyes and lowered his head, "I will try to get back when I can." He left, never to return.

Mother sobbed and wept for weeks. Seeing her that way shattered me. My childhood heart broke. My father cared for my mother in his own way. But his duties, desires, and restless nature overpowered him. How do I forgive him for abandoning my mother with nine children? She clung to the hope that they would reunite, a fragile illusion to keep the pain at bay.

In an instant, as if the tea knew, I was overwhelmed by the emotions of all three of us in that scene. A luminous sphere hovered over my heart, carrying the missing fragment of myself. As it merged back into me, I gasped, clutching my chest. The vision faded, and I found myself slumped on the temple floor, sweating, nauseous, and gasping for breath.

"Relax as much as possible," Artemis said. "I had a feeling it was about Zeus.

"How?" I said, trying to realign with my senses.

"You spoke his name more than once. Many of us have had to heal the father wound and our distant ties with Zeus." Artemis went to the table to make another tea. "This tea will quicken your healing. I recommend you to rest for a while."

Part IV – Integrating a New Story

The following week, Artemis welcomed a few visitors; Daphne, Arethusa, and several other Nymphs. Each possessed a wild and untamed spirit and shared tales of their trials and transformations, weaving laughter and channeling wisdom.

Arethusa introduced herself to me. "How are you doing Calliope?"

"Better than anticipated. Have we met?"

"Yes, it was by a spring on Helikon."

"Oh?"

"I was the spring at the time, my prior form. You sang beautifully to me; it's hard to forget a voice like yours."

I blushed. "Artemis, do you still have that tea? Excuse me." I smiled and darted off, pulling Artemis aside. "What are you doing?"

"Shhh, you need company and stories. It's for your healing," Artemis assured.

"What type of healing?" I asked.

"You're enjoying yourself. Arethusa is the wisest of the Nymphs, and you two have much in common. Wait until you hear her sing."

I relaxed. "You're right. Arethusa is charming. There's no harm in talking to her."

"It is going to take time to integrate Calliope. Things don't change overnight, even for the Gods. Be grateful you're not a mortal."

We spent several more weeks swimming, dancing, singing, sharing stories, and cooking, activities that nourish a Muse. But deep down, I knew my time was waning.

"Next week, I have to leave and travel to Aoede's. It's a long overdue visit," I explained.

Artemis unclasped the sapphire locket from her neck. "Thank you for letting me wear this; it has been healing to the forest. You should consider inviting a few Nymphs to accompany you. I'll make my way to your lands when the time allows."

"I agree, but the pirate will require extra silver."

"Consider it done," Artemis shrugged.

We made our way down the mountain to the plaza, where the pirate and his crew were busy loading the ship for the voyage home.

Andrea waved and chuckled, "You're a month late, Calliope, but I knew you would show. You sent payment to me."

"You're well, Andrea."

"This isle has such feasts! I overindulged." He tapped his belly.

"I do have a favor to ask. A few friends will be joining me. Do you happen to have any extra cabins available?"

"Yes, yes, I will have one of the crew bunk with me."

I nodded and boarded the ship with three undercover Nymphs.

Part V – In Deep Waters

"You brought Nymphs aboard this ship? By the Gods!" said Andrea, shaking with a sword at Erasinos's neck.

"Lady, has illness taken you?! We'll end up at the bottom of these waters if you let them roam free on the deck."

"Steady, Andrea, steady. Let's not be brash." I kept my attention on him and gestured to Arethusa and Meliae.

The Nymphs sang a hypnotic melody into the room. One by one, the crew succumbed to sleep. Andrea struggled to hold on, but his grip faltered. The sword slipped from his hand and clattered to the floor as he collapsed to his knees before sprawling unconscious.

"So, do any of you know how to steer a ship?" The Nymphs shook their heads, speechless. Humph.

We secured the crew and laid them out on the deck, leaving one sailor at the helm to steer. Andrea wrestled against his bindings and motioned for me to come closer. I hesitated, untying the gag from his mouth.

"What have you done?!" he cried.

I could tell he was visibly shaken. "What's troubling you, Andrea?" My voice was softer as his mind was lost in fear.

"Countless crews have fallen under the Nymph's lull. It ends with broken ships."

I studied the group, sipping tea and calmly sitting in a circle.

"They are harmless to me. Maybe some sailors antagonized the wrong Nymphs?"

Andrea watched, "They don't like us."

"You are the ones that don't like them."

As I stood, the sun dipped lower, and an icy draft prickled my neck, yet it was only early afternoon, with not a single cloud in sight.

Andrea's eyes widened with shock and fear.

Turning, I faced a nightmare from the water's depths. An eel-like creature with a monstrous coiling body loomed over us with eyes molten red. Its obsidian-scaled body prowled in a sinuous motion and lashed its tail at the bow of our ship. The wood splintered under the immense pressure, and cracks rang out as the beast tightened its grip.

Before I could reach them, the Nymphs had already leaped beneath the water. I lunged to the side, gripping the rail as the ship lurched. Arethusa, Erasinos, and Meliae surfaced, their arms cutting through the waves as they gestured to cover our ears. Scrambling across the deck, I ripped at the bindings of the crew, shouting.

"Don't listen! Whatever you do, don't listen!"

The Nymphs unleashed a shrill across the sea, shaking the ship and boiling the water. The creature thrashed and convulsed as the song took hold. It lashed out but soon grew sluggish and disoriented, screeching with rage as the Nymphs sang. With a final surge, the monstrous eel whipped forward and hurled itself toward the deck. The crew scurried. Its last wail fell silent as its red eyes dimmed, and it slipped back into the rough sea.

The crew cheered, but the relief in their voices did nothing to ease the tight knot in my chest. I scanned the water, choking back tears, afraid the Nymphs had been taken with the beast. Exhausted, I searched the waters for hours, but they were nowhere to be found. As night deepened, I remained vigilant, anxiety gnawing at me.

Andrea approached in disbelief. "I didn't understand. What the Nymphs just did—I thought we were doomed. I owe them an apology." His voice was uneasy. "I owe you."

Saddened and grief-stricken, I crawled into bed and didn't come out for days.

O! AKOUEL! The dog began to bark again.

Landfall already? I thought heavy-heartedly. *We should turn the ship around and find the Nymphs.*

I climbed to the top deck and spotted the Nymphs laughing with the dog. Staggering across the deck, joy tangled with sorrow inside me from their absence.

"What happened?!"

"We elected to give the creature an intervention. The creature felt misunderstood. No one was listening." Arethusa concluded. "And we hypnotized him to stop harming ships," Erasinos said brightly. Arethusa ribbed Erasinos with an elbow.

"Don't leave again without a word, okay?" I whispered to Arethusa, hugging her tight. "I thought you were gone."

Arethusa's voice, though bright, carried the weight of the ocean's wisdom. They weren't just trying to protect us and calm a creature that lost its way.

The captain was so grateful to the Nymphs that he gave them free passage on the ship whenever they desired. Andrea approached me after the excitement. "So that's what the storm conjured. I've never encountered such a sea creature in these waters. Are the Gods angry with us?

Part VI – The Storyteller's Pen

I awoke early and watched Arethusa sleep. Delicately, I smoothed back her dark hair from her Goddess-like face. She was thousands of years old but not a day over 33 in mortal years. She must be exhausted from helping the struggling creature and swimming for that many days.

Slipping on my robe and touching the sapphire locket, I felt it humming. Since the return voyage, the necklace's essence has grown stronger. Perhaps Aunt Aoede has the answers.

We made landfall a few days ago and parted ways with Andrea. It was bittersweet, but I promised to reunite for another adventure.

I felt reluctance; home offered comfort but not the clarity sought. Luckily, the Nymphs kept Mother distracted. After several days, I announced my plans. Mother was in high spirits. "Yes, it is far overdue. Your aunt could use the company, and she loves the Nymphs. Honestly, why doesn't she visit us more?"

Having had our fill of sea life, the Nymphs and I agreed to travel by horseback instead. After bidding the family farewell, I walked into the yard and found the Nymphs attempting to ride a horse. One sat backward, another had no saddle, and Arethusa, the only one facing the right direction, held no reins. Instead, she spoke into the horse's ear, which, not to my surprise, listened to her.

"Have any of you actually ridden a horse?"

"I have seen other people ride horses," said Meliae. "How hard can it be?"

"Why do they have to have straps around them? Why don't we ask the horse to go to Aoedes," Erasinos inquired.

Euterpe and Polyhynmia walked by concerned but were encouraging. After an hour of lessons and ensuring everyone was seated and comfortable, we set off to the south. Aunt Aoede adores the warmer climate and sunlit beaches.

"Meliae, you have to tell the horse to go. Make a cluck sound," I said.

"Oh, now we talk to the horse! "Cluck, cluck," Meliae said with exaggerated drama.

The terrain was rougher than I remembered, with canyons, hidden coves, rocky hills, steep inclines, and waterfalls carved into the landscape. Still, we made a reasonable distance and found a cave to shelter in for the night. While the Nymphs gathered wood and tended to the horses, I arranged a circle of stones and sang the fire awake. I watched the flames against the cave walls. Weariness crept in, and I rested my head.

"Calliope, Calliope, you can awaken." With voices in unison, I knew it was the Five Ancient Ones.

I made my way to a stone in the circle.

"Muse, your story is only beginning, and many tasks are ahead of you. Your Aunt Aoede has forgotten about the magical item that must be gifted to you."

"I will remind my aunt. What are these other tasks you speak about?"

"You will start your work in the middle realm. Mortals are complex, but you will learn their ways. You cannot inspire them like some Gods, Faeries, or Nymphs. They must eat and sleep. Their bodies will require breaks on occasion. They are denser than we are accustomed to being."

"That sounds complicated."

"We all have faith you will do fine. Remember to ask your aunt. Get some rest, Calliope."

Do we need more branches for the fire?

I lifted my head and turned to Arethusa. "Yes, it's useful for the evening. We'll bring the rest of the kindling with us."

Arethusa sat beside me. "You're preoccupied."

"Yes, I am anticipating the meeting with Aunt Aoede, and maybe it's from being the firstborn," I half-jokingly stated.

Seven days later, we arrived. Perched atop a southern hill overlooking the ocean, her home sat beside a thriving spring. We led the horses to drink and made our way to her cottage.

Before I could knock, she swung open the door. "Darlings! All of you are welcome! Welcome!" She wore a flowing floral robe with soft slippers. Thick curls sprung around her angelic features.

"Did you catch wind that we were coming?" I laughed.

My aunt, unlike my mother or her other sister, Melete, had a whimsical memory: present but never too fixed in place.

"Of course, Of course!" She moved out of the way, revealing the Fates standing behind her. "Some messengers came through the area this week and mentioned your arrival!"

My aunt was thrilled to have so many guests. Like my mother, she loved to entertain. In the midst of all the festivities, I joined in so much that I almost lost track of time...and forgot to ask her about the magical object. Finally, I pulled her aside.

"Yes, yes, take two moments," she said, singing.

"I received a visit from these Five Ancient Ones, seated in a circle. Do you remember them?"

"I do, I do—they are funny and powerful Storytellers. Although it was not fun being in a circle with them. They work too much if you ask me."

"Why did you leave?"

"A Muse and Faerie are required to sit in the Storyteller circle. It is part of the Divine plan, and I don't have all the details. But I did my years of service and took my leave, like your mother. It was a powerful time, with many long nights and days. Don't let them run you out of inspiration, okay?"

"I won't. I can sense these Storytellers have changed the way they do things. They mentioned you have a magical item that will help me with my work in the middle realm?"

"Yes, yes, of course! I have what you need...or rather, what was for the next Muse called upon, which is you! Now, let me think...where did I put it? Give me a moment to sort through these rooms."

"As long as it's ready before we depart for home in a few weeks."

"I'll have it ready for you," she said, wandering off while talking to herself about where she'd seen it last.

She called back, "Oh! I have information about that sapphire locket you're wearing; don't let me forget!"

"Okay!" I yelled back. Chuckling, I set out to find the Fates.

"We don't meddle in what you Muses do," Atropos said, her voice steady and firm. We can't lay out every step of your path. It wouldn't be fair. You must learn, adapt, and grow in your own way. As much as we adore you and as much as I cherish my role as your Godparent, we are bound by a sacred vow. Some things must unfold as they are meant."

I had asked them about the call of the Five Ancient Ones, and their response was unsurprising. I gazed out at the endless ocean and cycling tides. With a sigh, I asked, "What is the Divine plan, anyway?"

"We don't have the entire story of what that is and can only assume. We have come to accept that we are as much in the equation as the mortals," said Lachesis. Here we were, Goddesses without answers, playing our role.

The following day, Aunt Aoede burst into my room, twirling with excitement as she flung open the curtains. "Calli, Calli, I found it! By the Fates!"

I pulled the covers over Arethusa and myself.

"Okay, okay, aunt, can I meet you in the study in a minute?"

She froze. "Oh, yes, of course, of course." A blush rose to her cheeks as she composed herself, offered a gentle wave, and quietly shut the door.

"Are you saying it was lying on the chair in your room this morning?" I said.

"Yes, yes, the plot thickens, doesn't it!"

My instincts pointed to the Fates, but I chose not to spoil the mystery for her.

"In whatever way it has appeared!" She said with glee.

She walked to a shelf, carefully selected a book, and cradled it as if it were the most precious thing in the world, then delicately placed it in my hands.

I grasped the ancient, leather-bound book, surprised by its remarkably pristine condition. The script on the cover predated recorded history.

"Go on, go on, open it," she said, with clasped hands.

As I opened the cover, a brilliance spilled into the room. The energy tingled against my skin. On one side, a glowing blank page. On the other, a magical gold quill nestled within the pages, its feather sparkling with stardust.

"It doesn't need ink; it flows continuously and effortlessly," Aunt Aoede said.

"Am I to give this to a mortal for a time?" I asked.

"Mercy, no, no! It might drive them mad!" she exclaimed, her eyes wide with urgency. "Well, I can only speculate what would happen if it fell into mortal hands. As a Muse of Storytelling, this book is one of your sacred tools. When you write within its pages, your words are transmitted into thought, appearing in the minds of those ready to receive them. Mortals call it Divine inspiration or listening to the Gods or something. That is what I remember.

Now, let's go over the Sapphire locket. It is another mysterious and powerful magical relic. No one can say who created it. Not even the Fates," she whispered. "Legend has it that a piece of the universe at its birth is embedded in the sapphire along with the original voice of Source itself."

"What does it do?"

"Its secrets remain elusive, even to us. The Fates and I have experimented with the locket. We know it has a healing effect on whoever wears it, enhancing their natural talents. But its purpose, again speculating, is to channel the

Divine voice to the world. The wearer gains remarkable eloquence, and over time, the locket's essence imprints upon them, even long after it is taken off."

"So your singing voice was forever changed?"

"Yes, I can sing in higher registers. My words land at the perfect moment, and simply speaking can soothe or even captivate both mortals and Gods," Aunt Aoede beamed.

No wonder her list of suitors never ends. Unlike my father, my aunt remained fully present and devoted to all her relationships.

"I'm excited to hear what you discover as its keeper. Now, let's see what the Nymphs have baked in the kitchen."

"Wait, you left them alone?" I said, panicking.

"Of course!"

Part VII – Ending are Beginnings

The weeks passed. Arethusa and I packed the last of our belongings. With our plans set, we said our farewells to Aunt Aoede and the Fates.

"Aunt Aoede, please visit us. Mother would love to see you," I said.

"I will, and I need to check in with a few people in your area. We can discuss how things are going with the book, pen, and locket," she said, holding my hands.

Atropos embraced me and offered advice: "If you encounter high winds and they blind you, continue the course, Calliope. Use your words. The locket will help."

"We will visit again next season and bring Aoede," Lachesis said.

Back on our horses, we waved goodbye before setting off north.

"I loved meeting Aoede. She is like a Nymph! I feel sad leaving." said Arethusa

"She doesn't handle goodbyes well. They make her ill, which might be why she doesn't visit often. Perhaps that's why the Fates were there, to help her through."

"When are we going back?" Erasinos chimed in.

"She will visit us in the north, Erasinos. It's been Fated."

We laughed.

The weather was mostly in our favor on the journey home until we neared a day's ride. The winds shifted from the north, pushing against us and delaying our trek home. The sky darkened, and thunder rumbled, shaking the terrain as lightning crackled with continuous strikes between Earth and Sky. Our hair stood on end from the static charge.

"I feel an unsettling sensation," said Meliae.

"This is not a good omen," said Arethusa, "It's not a great sign when that happens to Meliae. Stay vigilant."

A relentless roar from the storm slammed into us, making it nearly impossible to ride. Branches were ripped from the trees, whipping past as an impenetrable shadow engulfed us. In the next flash of lightning, a glowing God emerged, lit like a star against the storm. His eyes filled with thunderbolts, his expression turbulent.

Zeus called Arethusa. "Nymph, you were to remain as the river you were transformed into. Who has undone this magic?" He approached me. "What Goddess are you?"

"Has Zeus himself failed to recognize his own daughter, Calliope?"

Storyteller, Muse, you retain your own power. Why have you altered Arethusa? She is no longer as she was before.

Arethusa, visibly upset, steadied her horse next to me, "I am not going back, Calliope."

"Almighty Zeus, hear my plea, Arethusa is with me. I did not shape her rebirth; she was ready for it. Are stories not meant to be rewritten when they revisit us?"

I observed my father, and my stomach sank. He felt like a stranger. A wave of pity and sorrow surfaced. Our relationship was one of distance and loss.

"You can change the story with my mother if you choose. That power is yours," I declared.

Zeus lowered his head, his voice somber. "There has never been a day when Mneme was not in my thoughts. But my duty comes first, even at my own expense. To visit and then leave again would have only broken her heart many times. I watch from afar, but there is nothing to be done, Muse."

The wind started to calm, and the clouds broke.

Zeus turned to Arethusa, his voice booming. "Nymph, you may continue with this rebirth, but speak of this matter to no one. There is a balance that must be maintained."

Arethusa, still shaking, spoke—barely audible. "Yes."

"Calliope, if you can weave a new story for your mother, a story where she finds someone who can share in her joy, that is my only wish."

In another flash, he was gone, and the clouds dissipated.

Tears fell from my eyes. I have never spoken to my father. I might disagree with his decisions, but he loved Mneme.

Arethusa turned to the group. "Let's go before he changes his mind."

As we headed for home, the locket around my neck hummed, and the conversation with Zeus played over and over in my mind. I realized that, despite Zeus's mastery over storms and his great power, he was a victim of his own story, unable to change the course laid out before him. Even with the ability to wield thousands of thunderbolts, Zeus had no control over the one thing I did: storytelling. I could shape lives, influence destiny, and, most importantly, change the plot.

Home no longer felt the same. A part of me had changed and broke free inside. I told Mother about my relationship with Arethusa. She was genuinely happy that I had found someone and recognized that her desire for me to marry had never been about me. It had been her own longing to marry Zeus.

Late one night, under the light of the spring full moon, I sat at my desk, watching Arethusa as she slept. With deep calmness, I opened the Muse book and stared at the blank illuminated page. How quickly the realizations came. I now know that strength does not come from control or keeping things tucked away but from the power of the raw heart. Arethusa, in her vulnerability and openness, is a model for such influence. That's what this relationship is teaching me. It was clear that I was no longer bound by the will of Zeus or Mneme.

I am free and sovereign, and the quill held the power to shape and forge the life filled with love that had always been there, waiting to be expressed. All it needed was for me to write the words. For the first time, I truly understood the inspiration of Muse. Stories are more than tales. They are a spell, a movement, and create life.

I lifted the golden quill, nervous and excited, for I knew words could change everything.

> It was a charming day; the sun was inviting, and the trees were filled with spring flowers. Following the scent of cherry blossoms, Mneme wandered through a blooming field, where she noticed a powerful God from afar.
>
> A pulsation of love streamed from her heart, and a longing erupted. For one knows when they meet the Beloved. Happiness welled in them, forever changing their fate...

The Heroine's Journey

Life, what truths have I uncovered beyond familiar shores?
Have my goals, ambitions, and desires drifted beyond my grasp?
Are the things I gather shields and illusions of safety?
My pockets carry the weight of tears pressed into crumpled tissues

And what of the longing that whispers from the depths
A faint voice to adventure, stifled by fear?
Urging me into the realms of risk, shadows and loss
Plunged into the depths, falling between the worlds

An Abyss of self-doubt, turmoil and chaos
yet, by some twist of fate and fleeting grace
a single match lay waiting on the ground
if I strike it aglow, everything will transform

The fire revealed battles and beasts untamed
one by one, they dissolved and took flight
beneath my feet, a thread of light...waiting
I grasped it, pulling with all my might

Unraveling a hidden treasure, long forgotten
called out from a distance, ancient past
a keeper of tools, of stories, of wisdom
of love, of creation, and of making

I opened inside, ascended into its power
with all the songs never written or sung
and the keys to sense, to self, and purpose
integrating aspects of wounds and wisdom

An alchemical union, a balance of opposites
Guiding me beyond thought, beyond reason
now, entering into the pure waters of truth
A homecoming, a return, a life reborn.

Journey & Adventure of the Creative Self

"In this journey, we will explore your creative self and the adventure it seeks to tell. Get into a comfortable position," Calliope said, putting another log on the fire.

Take a deep breath in and out slowly. Let the weight of the day fade as you sink deeper into your body. With each breath, feel yourself becoming more relaxed. Find your edges; if you're not sure where they are, make it up. Journey deeper into your body and relax as you move further inward. (Pause)

In the distance, hear the gentle rhythm of the ocean entering your awareness. As you do, you become aware that you are on a ship. See the movements of the ocean waves rolling beneath you. Smell the crisp salt air and feel the cool mist from the waves touching your skin. Notice the atmosphere around you. Is the ocean calm, or are there large cresting waves? Does the sun warm your skin, or is it a breezy night beneath a sky full of stars?

What does the ship look like? Is it anchored? Who is steering? Does it have a crew? Find out. (Pause)

Somewhere on this ship is your creative self; see if you can locate them. When you find this part of yourself, ask: Where is the vessel heading? Is it a new destination or your home? Ask them their name, and get curious. Learn more about them. (Pause)

Ask your creative self what they need in order for you to thrive and flourish. How can you support them? (Pause)

Begin to finish up your conversation, but before you go, your creative self gives you a gift for the months ahead. (Pause)

Offer them a gift of gratitude. Then, begin to float upward, leaving the ship and returning to your body. Come back to the room and open your eyes.

A Journey With the Storyteller

"We are traveling on a second journey. This time into the realm of story." Calliope said. *"Sit or lay in a comfortable position."*

Expand into your body. Bring your attention to your feet. With another breath, start to expand and allow this sensation and feeling to continue to move out and around you. In the background, you begin to hear the ocean waves. Feel the warm sand beneath your feet as you stroll along the beach. Continue walking along the shoreline to a clearing, where a warm fire burns with seats arranged around it. Find a place to sit and relax.

As you watch the horizon, you notice a twinkle of light far out at sea, drawing closer. A group of horses swiftly gallop over the water, striding and gliding in unison with a celestial light. One horse with an illuminated figure charges ahead, approaching the shore at full chariot speed.

As they draw closer, you recognize the Storyteller. The horse slows to a stop, and the Storyteller gracefully dismounts, taking a seat beside you by the inviting fire.

"You've arrived at an extraordinary place. The greatest stories ever shared have unfolded around a great fire, bathed in moonlight," the Storyteller explains.

"This is a gateway to the inner realm. Within you live stories from the oral tradition, passed down through generations. They carry the essence of who you are, your triumphs, losses, and mysteries. Every story is a lesson, a reflection of history and culture. Every word spoken, every poem written, every tale dreamt is a spell. Storytellers carry the power to bring us closer to healing and reconnection with our souls."

She pauses, and you both listen to the fire crackle and pop.

"Your whole being and existence is a story. You are made from stories, this life, and others. Everything that happens seeks to resolve itself in you and in the collective."

She reaches into her bag and pulls out a glowing and alive magical pen. She hands it to you, along with a piece of paper.

"Write a sentence about the most extraordinary thing you've learned in this lifetime." (Pause)

When you have finished, return the piece of paper to the Storyteller.
She smiles. "Gods and mortals like their stories," she says. "And we shall continue to tell them."

She reaches back into her bag and reveals another pen specially made for you. If it feels right, accept it and ask her questions. (Pause)

Thank the Storyteller and offer her a gift of gratitude. Now, sit back, listen to the fire, close your eyes, take a few deep breaths, and begin to come back to your body.

Calliope's Well-Wish

On this ship of life, you may encounter many things on your path: calm waters, tumultuous waves, great storms, and mirages. At times, you may drift, or the winds may guide your sail. Know that you are always at home within yourself.

Embrace the journey and the tale of life; fear not the waves at sea.
When you feel or hear that longing and call for adventure,
do not let it pass you by; let it grow within you and take flight.
Be open to the knowing voice, trust life and the one it seeks you to have.

It knows the direction to carry you, surrender to the living and your rebirth.
Let everything go and live the most extraordinary story ever told.
You.

Much love and many adventures,
Calliope

Chapter XII
Polyhymnia: Muse of Sacred Hymns

"A hymn is not just a song but an offering, a moment of connection between the mortal and the Divine." —Plato

Hurrian Hymn No. 6

*"While you live, shine
Have no grief at all
Life exists only for a short while
And time demands its toll."*

Hymn is to Nikkal
Goddess of orchards in Semitic
Syria, 1,400 BCE
The world's earliest melody

I WALKED IN SILENCE SINCE ARRIVING BACK FROM THE MUSE OF STO-
RYTELLING. Ella noticed and caught up with me. "I apologize," she
said, her voice thoughtful. "The Hall is a reflection of the mind. What
you see around you, the external world is a mirror, of what lies within. Our
thoughts and emotions shape reality. I can only guide you to experience and
witness your limitations. But it is your inner realm that has to transform."

"Ella, not every wound or tendency has cleared its way out. Are we still not
growing and working through triggers and patterns, even after significant
openings and realizations?"

"Yes. Even as a Wayfinder, I still have things to overcome. Anyone embodied
will encounter challenges, no matter how far along one's journey. There are
resistances and old tendencies, but they do subside, though it takes seeing
and dedication. Be patient with yourself, Grace. Now, let us go inward. Focus
on the path. Do not let these distractions claim any more of your space. We
are venturing to Polyhymnia, Muse of the Sacred Hymns. We will need to
go this way."

We proceeded, moving in silence, immersed in a reflective state. I became
aware of the rhythm of my breath, the soft exhale between footsteps. My ears
buzzed, and my heart grew louder, reverberating through my chest. Truth
permeated me. We each inherited the simple presence of our breath, our
steps, and our pulse.

Ella stopped and made a sweeping gesture toward a towering staircase.

"You will need to climb these stairs. At the top is the passage to Polyhymnia,
the gateway to what you seek."

A mountain of stairs snaked upward, winding high into the sky. There was
no handrail for support. *The Hall must know I don't like heights.* My palms
began to sweat. I placed my foot on the first tread, then the next, each step
taking me higher. The thought of my parents crossed my mind. I missed
them, and the days we wouldn't have together. I remembered my last conversation with my father, how he'd bought tickets to Rome to surprise Mom.
Tears streamed down my cheeks, and the ache in my legs pulled me back to
the present. Still, I pressed on. Reaching the top, breathless, I stood before
a white door covered in ancient symbols. I knocked and turned the handle.

Within, there was a well-tended garden dappled with flowers and olive trees. The air shimmered with a golden mist, dissipating as the sun began its rise, casting warmth over the scene like a Turner painting brushed with touches of Monet. I meandered past clusters of lilies, their delicate petals bowing and waving in the wind. I heard a casual humming. Rounding the next hedge, I saw a statuesque woman tending the honeysuckle, gathering its ripe blossoms.

"Hello, Grace," she said, continuing her work. "There's a bench a short distance over there where I'll meet you." She pointed.

Finding the bench, I rested, taking in the greenscape. Polyhymnia arrived in a long, bright blue robe with a fitted hat resting over her curly brunette hair. She was the quintessential Priestess, calm and composed, radiating strength and full of presence. She was familiar, but I could not place her.

"I see you are enjoying the garden," she said.

"It's gorgeous. It's as if magic itself lives here."

"This is where I am most at home," she said, settling into herself. After a long reflection, Polyhymnia spoke.

"I could feel your disrupted thoughts as you entered."

"Many emotions have surfaced. Long-hidden patterns have emerged throughout my journey with each Muse, especially around my parents' passing, and my sense of belonging and purpose," I said.

"Perhaps you find these things unfavorable because they feel unpleasant, which is common. Maybe you could begin to see these patterns as gifts to clear your Being?"

I sat listening with my eyes fixed on the ground.

"Let my words be the bridge between us, Initiate. Let these trees and flowers calm your spirit. Let the hymns of the deep forest and the songs of the vast oceans sing to you. Let my words uplift you like an elixir for your soul."

"I am the One of many hymns," her voice dropped into a rhythmic pace. "Let these sacred words open your heart to longing, to the connection of all that is true."

"May they bring light and dissolve illusions. May they expand life into you and awaken your devotion. These Muse hymns destroy the old and give way to the new. These songs draw and encourage you to wholeness. From a distant shore, these sacred words call you home, to awaken, to reach beyond the possible, and to live."

When I speak this voice into the infinite field of love and wisdom, I reach through time and space, through doubt, into pure oneness. I am the movement of the voice, channeling what must be heard. I am the Divine Poet of Mysteries.

Surrender to these hymns and let them resonate within. Let them change you, rebuild you, and strengthen your resilience. Let these words shake awake your inner power. Hear them, and wrap yourself in their velvety comfort. Gather back to your vessel and purify it, for it is the meeting place of Earth and stars. Merge inward with what quenches your truth. Drink deeply from my well, surrender, and surrender, and surrender…

Muse of the Priestess

I live within her as a dreamy poet
reflecting her inner landscape
and live between many worlds
in the background, unnoticed
listening to every prayer

The Muse's gift of prophecies
surrender, and devotional hymns
my holy songs, sing aloud,
chanting the Earth realm sacred

Inquiring and inspiring, I ask
What are you devoted to?
What do you embrace in life?
How can you surrender even more?

Who can answer these
or stand on the precipice of change
and open the gates of mystery?

To surrender to life
in every moment, to step forward
even when existence is bleak
when grief or tragedy strikes,
or when death visits

How does one gather the pieces
and voice praise or song
How does one tend
that forever hymn of life

How does one sing of love
What do you offer its affection?
How do you care for its garden?
What story has it written in your life?
Drop the layers of learning,

the traumas and fears
dive into the depths
Of the sacred song to transport you
beyond limitations to the sacred

Devotion is for the fearless,
the courageous, and the daring
who are willing to live its truth.

Reborn from Exile

We listened to the wind mingle through the trees while the larks spoke their morning tales. *"Let me share some of my story and how I began my journey as Muse,"* Polyhynmia said.

Part I – Along a Distant Tide

This garden was planted long before many of your lifetimes, after my training with Aunt Meletes. She took me in as a child to begin my training as a Muse of Sacred Hymns. My aunt is kind, disciplined, and unwavering. She is nurturing in her own way, but training came first, with countless hours dedicated to practice. Each morning and most evenings, we sat in silence. At times, I would sit alone for days. I scarcely spent time with my sisters, only joining them for occasional celebrations. When not in practice, we spent time in her library. We pored over ancient texts on magical principles and the songs of Source and unraveled the hymns passed down to us from the Titans and beyond.

One rainy morning, after a sleepless night, a voice filled the room. It chanted from my lips, a majestic expression that sang healing into the world. Sound and hours slipped away. My body lightened, drifting through planes of existence. I journeyed further into a place with no beginning or end, a lightscape that encompassed all things in a state with the most sublime sounds.

The return felt abrupt. My aunt touched my head, guiding me back to the middle realm. "You have been gone for over a week in the outer celestial world. It's time to proceed to the next phase of learning."

We began my immersion with the elements of Gaea. As I spoke, the wind sang, the sea shifted her tides, the rocks told me their ancient stories, and fire lit my entire body. At the core of it all, I became the spirit of inspiration, recognizing that each element carries its own life, love, and purpose. I existed within these elements, and they, in turn, lived within me. Unfolding in my own time were countless songs and lyrics for invocation. That is how I began to initiate into the Muse of Sacred Hymns.

But let me tell a story I hold dear to this day: my travels, which carried me from the creative gates of the Minoans to an ancient Phoenician route leading east. My training with Melete had finished, and the land near Ur beckoned me. For several seasons, I lived alone at the border of the desert and the fertile alluvial plain near the banks of the Pruattu River. I met a Priestess, torn from her homeland, exiled by fate.

There, one evening, as I rested beneath the twilight sapphire sky, I felt the rise of the summer new moon. Flashes of heat and distant lightning branched low along the skyline. The scent of burning pine drifted on the breeze as tall green grass wavered and ruffled in the wind. Guided by my senses, I crossed the field toward the tidal line. My gaze was drawn to a fire across the river, where a woman knelt, offering prayers to the flames. I listened to her cries of sorrow as she called out to Inanna.

A flush of heat and tingles quickened my hands and heart. A sign the Muse was being called to help this woman. Delving deeper within, I whispered words of power to the water. With my feet on the river and my mind in deep focus, the path revealed itself to me.

The woman, taken aback and trembling with grief, wiped her tears. As I reached the other side, she fell to her knees and addressed me.

"Oh, illuminated One! What Being you are! I have petitioned you, Goddess. Have you heard my plea? Please take me away from this place, for my work is done!"

"I have heard your tears. What has brought you to this state, Sacred Keeper?

"The home I once knew has been torn away, exiled into the unknown. The temple of my dedication is gone. I am without belonging. King Sargon has passed. As his daughter, my presence and role hindered a fluctuating structure. I lament that the fields will wither without ceremonies, and the rain will be sparse. Who will tend the inner garden of life?" "I am Enheduanna 𒀭𒊩𒌆𒉌, Priestess of Inanna."

I felt the weight of abandonment and deep despair, yet her devotion and heart burned with intensity. Though exhausted, she shined with life. This was a human who had touched the very core of their inner power.

"Priestess, I am Polyhymnia. Your cause of concern is recognized. Allow me to ease your matter for a moment." With a sign and gesture to the wind, the hymn I sang drifted into the Priestess and calmed her to sleep. I sat in reflection of her plight.

Part II – The First Priestess

The morning sun welcomed us. Enheduanna stirred awake.

"How long have I been asleep? This rest has comforted me."

"Two days."

She gathered herself, walked to the river, and stared at her reflection. "I am still here."

"Enheduanna, there is more work to be done. Has Inanna not spoken to you of such endeavors? Has she not taken you to the furthest reaches of the Underworld for transformation?"

"As a Priestess, I have participated in Inanna's ceremonies, which deeply shaped both my inner and outer journey. I've had to release many layers, including the role I once knew. But since the exile...my senses have changed. My connection is weak."

"You are in the Underworld now and with struggle. I offer you a ritual at sunset to invoke Inanna for the wisdom you seek. I will hold space as a guide for you."

Enheduanna looked across the landscape. "I don't have the proper offerings for such a ritual! How can we invoke the Goddess like this?"

"Your training has been gifted to you. But this exile, this life apart from your structured world, calls for your devotion and surrender. It asks you to empty yourself. Your task is to rest your duties of healing others for a time. You need nourishment. Where are those who have accompanied you?"

She gestured beyond the trees. "An assembly is close by the riverside. How shall I introduce you?"

"Make no mention of my origins, for their path blooms in another direction."

"Goddess, your eyes are ion, and your otherworldliness may be addressed."

"We can figure that out on the way," I said.

We gathered the Priestess's belongings, cleared the ground, and made our way through the trees to the caravan. A guard nodded and saluted to Enh duanna. Several elaborate wool tents stood around a central fire and an outdoor kitchen. Two Priestesses saw us and immediately approached, bowing.

"Enheduanna, you've been gone for days. We were preparing to send the guard."

"Yes, there is no need for concern, and my apologies for worrying you. I needed some time alone for a day or two to figure out our next steps, and I have found an answer. Polyhymnia is conducting a ceremony this evening, but it must be done across the river. She is visiting from a remote region of Delos.

Please find Ninti ✳ ◁〗⊣⟨✳ to accompany me on this occasion. We'll eat, then pack a few things."

Part III – Invoking the Goddess

We waited at the river's edge as the first stars emerged, preparing to cross. "Where is the reed for passage?" asked Ninti.

"Be still, Ninti; we will walk with Polyhymnia."

Ninti looked bewildered. I moved my fingers in a weaving motion, calling an incantation to the river and blending with the water. Opening the connection, I glided forward, walking across the waterway as if it were solid earth. I reached out my hands to Enheduanna and Ninti, their eyes wide with awe.

"Don't look down into the water. It may make you dizzy," I whispered from my centered state. My focus had to remain clear, not just for myself, but to steady them as well.

Ninti closed her eyes while Enheduanna viewed the other side with courage. "It's like we are walking on stars, almost floating," said Enheduanna.

Ninti peeked with one eye, then snapped it shut. "Tell me when we've reached the other side."

As our feet touched solid ground, we crossed the field toward my dwelling. I turned to the Priestesses.

"There will be plenty of space here for the ritual. Beyond the tent is a warm spring. Take these robes and purify yourselves while I prepare."

Ninti turned to Enheduanna as they walked away. "What kind of Priestess training do they have in Delos?"

Though the ritual had yet to begin, I already felt the tremors of love and fear within both Enheduanna and myself. Calling such a sacred Goddess was a powerful act; the Priestess had to surrender enough to allow her to arrive and support the connection. There was a chance she might not come.

I chanted while drawing a sacred circle in the sand inscribed with the text Melete had taught me. I finished with Inanna's symbol, the eight-pointed star of her domain, drawing it for the invocation. At the center of the star is an upright, empty vessel, symbolizing the space of potential. Each corner held a representation of one of the elements. Rugs and cushions, acquired from local merchants weeks ago, were placed around for comfort. To purify the area, sesame oil lamps were used, and a blend of myrrh and cinnamon incense was lit. I finished preparing the ritual space by laying out fresh herbs and warm stones alongside the blankets.

The Priestesses returned from their purification, each draped in a red ritual robe, their waists adorned with gold and white cloth belts. I invited them to sit on the cushions at the center, offering chalices filled with water from a Muse spring. Sensing they were entering a shifted state, I sat with my drum and continued guiding them inward.

Speaking to the sky, I stated our intention. "We are petitioning the Goddess Inanna to join our ritual for guidance. A circle of protection has been cast, and the elements hold and guard the edges."

Enheduanna, her voice laden with distress, spoke her words: "Goddess Inanna, Sacred Love of the Worlds, hear my plea. I seek guidance in this exile. What is the role of this one to become?"

The rhythm of my drumming grew louder, and a loving hymn erupted from deep within me. Enheduanna and Ninti soon joined, their voices merging with the chant.

Inanna—ahh, Inanna—ahh,
Sacred Beloved,
Inanna—ahh, Inanna—ahh,
Sacred Beloved,
Oh! Inanna—ahh

Come to me, sing into me,
Through the night, open thee
Inanna—ahh, Inanna—ahh,
Sacred Beloved
Oh! Inanna—ahh

Come to me, renew me,
Life-giver, awaken me.
Inanna—ahh, Inanna—ahh,
Sacred Beloved
Oh! Inanna—ahh

A mist formed above the central clay vessel as our collective chant height-ened. It sparkled and unfurled like tendrils and streamed into Ninti's eyes, filling her with Inanna's light. I softened the beat of the drum, watching as Ninti's movements began to alter expression. She trembled and quivered. Her body surrendered as the Goddess's presence merged with hers.

Ninti shifted in posture and presence, her voice channeling the power of Inanna. "Enheduanna, Priestess, loving one, what has brought you to this plea and crisis?"

Enheduanna lowered her head and bowed as tears streamed from her charged eyes.""Beloved Goddess Inanna, I seek your guidance and direction in this exile."

"Priestess, what challenges you now is no exile but transformation. You are being emptied. Things within you are becoming undone. I sense barriers to your heart. Why have you denied yourself the true pleasures of living? The mortal world is in disarray due to your lack of trust in life. You have not all-owed life to unfold in its own time and way. You are living in resistance. You are stepping into a sacred fire. Allow it to move its way through you. This is not forever. It will recede when you rekindle your inner flame. Enheduanna, if you and this vessel (Ninti) are willing, I will apply the great rite of engage-ment to accelerate the way."

"Beloved Goddess, this great rite is understood and will allow this working with Ninti's consent," said Enheduanna.

Inanna moved aside to let Ninti speak. "Enheduanna and Goddess, I accept this ritual as an aspect and channel."

The Goddess Inanna settled back into Ninti's body. "Muse, continue the chant and drumming. Converse with me before I leave this vessel."

I agreed, and the drumbeat shifted, drifted, and strengthened, infusing the space with ecstatic energy. Enheduanna and the Goddess sat facing each other.

The Goddess lifted Ninti's hand, her vessel, and gently pressed it to Enheduanna's chest.

"Continue to breathe in and out," the Goddess said.

Enheduanna's eyes fluttered, her head falling back as she let out a moan that mingled pleasure with pain. Pressure built within her, breaking the blocks that had kept her stagnant, confused, and afraid.

"Don't hold on. Let go, my love," said the Goddess.

The Goddess's hand brushed through Enheduanna's hair, sliding to the back of her neck, guiding her closer. She slowly caresses Enheduanna with tenderness. Their lips met—Enheduanna leaned in, deepening the kiss. The ritual energy heightened, and passion intensified as the Goddess's fingers traced and lingered over Enheduanna's breasts. She embraced Enheduanna, her body pressing close as her legs slowly wrapped around her. The Goddess's lips glided along Enheduanna's soft neck, sending her into shivers as she eased open her gown, slipped it over her shoulders and whispered into Enheduanna's ear. The Goddess slowly loosened the knot of Enheduanna's robe, undressing her as if peeling away the layers of her former self. Their eyes locked, and their combined power swelled in Divine union. Their breath synchronized, becoming a rhythm of longing and transformation.

The drumbeat quickened as their cries reached a crescendo into a liberating freedom. Trembling, energy sprang from Enheduanna's heart and burst out the top of her crown. She cried in ecstasy as a shower of brightness lit the deep night.

As the expanded state subsided, Enheduanna collapsed into the Goddess's arms. The Goddess held and kissed her tenderly before laying her on the soft blankets.

Inanna turned to me. "Polyhymnia, I am deeply grateful for your support of this Priestess. I have been watching your training from afar. You have also been seeking direction. Allow me to amplify your gift, Muse."

I set the drum aside as she settled before me. She anchored herself to the ground and drew a white current of ethereal ribbons from the Earth. Luminous with lifeforce, Inanna touched my throat and head. Her activation traveled throughout my body, and vivid colors raced past my vision. My breath quickened. Sensations unlocked something hidden within me as my body surrendered.

"We will meet again, Muse." She pressed a lasting kiss to my lips and departed.

By morning, I felt grounded and renewed. The green field was amplified by the early light. The sun was brighter, the water louder, and the breeze sweeter.

Enheduanna and Ninti were eating quietly as they tidied the space. I could sense their transformation and ease. Both spoke softly, as if still held in the sacred.

"It was dream-like, but I don't remember much of anything," Ninti said. Unbeknownst to her, the aspect had changed her eyes into speckles of gold.

A faint star-shaped mark shimmered at the nape of Enheduanna's neck, invisible to most but not to those who had seen the light of Inanna.

"I do not walk in exile. I walk in flame," Enheduanna said, sparked with her inner power. In time, Enheduanna regained her role as High Priestess in her homeland of Ur. The Goddess re-ignited her devotion, and her spirit continued to blossom and unfold.

As the vision of the story faded, Polyhymnia rose from the garden bench. "Initiate, let's begin your next journey."

"What about Inanna?" I asked.

"It is a story for another time." She smiled.

The Exaltation of Inanna

Inanna, Queen of the Heavens,
I will sing your praises,
I will sing your exaltation!
You are the one who has no rival in the sky,
You are the one who is the great one in the heavens,
You are the light of the heavens and the earth!
You are the one who is adorned with the shining light,
You are the one who moves in the heavens like a storm!

Enheduanna, 𒀭𒊹𒉺𒀭𒄑
High Priestess, Poetess, Writer
Ur, 2200 BCE

A Journey of Purification & Delphi

"Initiate this is a two-part journey; the first is for purifying, and the second is with an Oracle." Said Polyhynmia.

Part I – Purification

Polyhymnia sits down beside you. "Gather yourself for this purification." Please find a comfortable position, whether sitting or lying down.

Begin to bring your awareness to your body, taking a few deep breaths in and out. Let your breath deepen, releasing any sounds naturally. Focus your attention on these sounds, whether external or internal. Go deeper and deeper, allowing yourself to relax even further. Expand your senses.

With your next breath, visualize or feel a bright flower-filled meadow before you. Sense and hear the wind gently fluttering through each leaf and flower. As it whistles over you, it carries its own sound. Listen. Smell. Hear the enchanting song of the nearby birds, singing to life.

Watch as they soar on the breeze overhead. As you take another breath, you find yourself in an old ancient-growth forest. The birds call your attention, and you follow them down a winding path. Notice the type of feathered friend you are following. Continue deeper into the forest, sensing and smelling how the surroundings change.

The forest path gradually transforms into an ancient road, leading you over weathered stones. Following around the next bend, you eventually arrive at a large, cooling pool nestled at the heart of an open temple. Take note of the time of day and the landscape.

At the pool, two Priestesses stand, holding fresh towels and incense containers that release the smoke of frankincense and myrrh. A sense of calm washes over you. One of the Priestesses gestures for you to move into the purifying bright blue water.

The Priestesses place the towels down and move to the far side of the temple, offering you privacy. Ease into the soothing, silky waters and allow them to revitalize your body and soul, purifying you completely. Mosaics and sacred symbols are along the pool walls and bottom. Notice which symbol draws your attention. For a moment, you submerge your head beneath the water. When you resurface, an illuminated Priestess stands at the other end. You feel her presence deeply. She lifts her head to the sky, singing in a barely audible tone.

The light begins to brighten in the sky; the rays of the sun and moon move around you, dancing across and through your body. Witness as the light removes your blocks and burdens, carrying them away. They float upward, where the sun's rays transmute them into light.

If it feels right, speak aloud what you wish to release. Gently allow the water to purify you. Take as much time as you need, and pay attention to what surfaces within you. (Pause)

The Priestess raises her hands to the sky once more, signaling the end of the purification. Turn inward and ask what your creative self requires. Listen closely. (Pause)

Finally, step out of the pool and gently dry yourself with the towels provided. Beside them, a fresh set of clothing is laid out for you. Notice its color and texture. What details stand out to you as you slip it on? You may leave your previous clothes behind by placing them in the sacred flames near the entrance or choose to bring them with you. Wave and leave the Priestesses an offering, then follow your feathered guide back along the path to where your journey began. (Pause)

Fully return to your body and the room. Gently open your eyes.

Part II – Delphi

"Settle in and relax as we journey inward to Delphi," Polyhymnia says, standing beside you.

Get into a comfortable position and bring your awareness to your body. Take a few deep breaths in and out, letting your breath deepen naturally and releasing anything you are holding on to right now. Focus on the sounds around you and within. With each breath, relax more deeply and surrender fully to this moment.

Begin by noticing your body, letting go of any tension as you exhale. Bring your attention to your feet. Expand into the sensation of the bottom of your feet upon a path. A gentle breeze stirs the air, carrying the scent of forest pine. Notice what surrounds you as you walk forward. As you round the next bend, a vast canyon stretches before you. A weathered rope ladder sways across a ravine. If you don't feel ready to cross, rest here.

If you are ready, venture onto the bridge and continue walking toward the other side. Take in the view and notice what is here. When you reach the other side, continue down the trail. You may see or hear flowers, plants, or animals as you walk.

The path curves again, revealing a clearing where distant ridges rise with clouds drifting across the sky. Before you, polished marble steps lead up to the ancient temple and the Oracle of Delphi. Make your way up to the heart of the temple. As you near, a soft hymn echoes off the stone walls, drawing you closer.

At the threshold, a Priestess stands patiently waiting. She gestures for you to enter. In a calm voice, she invites you to ask the Oracle any question about your life. Ascend the half-dozen steps into a narrow chamber and feel the vibration of the sacred space. Witness the gentle mist rising from the earth. Before you, the Oracle. She says your name and tells you that she has been expecting you. She is ready to answer your questions. Take your time and listen to her guidance. (Pause)

Take a few more moments to finish your conversation. (Pause)

When you are ready, express your gratitude and offer a gift or gesture of thanks to the Oracle. Then, retrace the path down the stairs, where the Priestess waits with one final gift. (Pause)

Focusing on your throat chakra, she sends healing energy to dissolve any blockages. She then sings a melody that soothes your spirit, clears away doubts, and offers you a symbolic object, something for the path ahead. In return, offer your gratitude and appreciation. (Pause)

Begin your return by descending the marble steps and following the path back across the bridge, around the bend, and back down the path. When you reach the original place of entry, draw your focus into your body and room. When you are ready, gently open your eyes.

The Cords of Delphi

With each pluck of the lyre, A Muse
Nete, the lowest note of the deep heart
Mese, living the middle note of expression
Hypate, the highest inspiration from above

She took a long breath, filling her lungs
Below the tripod, smoke rose to greet her
The air, saturated with an ecstatic charge
of magic, of mystery, and of the sacred

Spirit called and invoked within the temple
The Oracle of Delphi, full and enlivened
Sang out and professed to the one before her
The Seeker awakened in trance

The pilgrim stepped before the Oracle
Priests blessed and accepted each gift
And tended to the Priestesses' voice
writing and scribing the words of the Divine

The Priestess rocked forward
foresight into the pilgrim's question
to the traveler's left, three Muses of Delphi
illuminated alongside the Seeker

Witnessing this, the Oracle spoke
before leaning back and closing her eyes

"Blessings are bestowed, and Grace to you traveler,
many lives she is.

Muses of song and of three called few lovingly,
inspired with the soul-sees.

A far and empty past found in you, spring is late,
yet does sing life anew.

You of the starry eyes, clair of mind within,
Thyself will be known."

Polyhymnia's Well-Wish

"The most remarkable devotion is to your inner self. Let every creative act become a devotion. I offer you this chant and passage Initiate."

May you surrender to life and allow it to bring you all its precious gifts
May you surrender to all Beings, for they are your greatest teachers
May you surrender inward so it will awaken you from your illusions
May you surrender to the infinite One so it may shower you with its wisdom
Turn toward what comes to you in life with grace; it will bring you inner
union and power.

Infinite love and blessings,
Polyhymnia

Chapter XIII
Urania: Muse of Astrology,
Prophecy & Future

"Some bloom by the radiant sun and others at night, in the quiet, under the full moon." —J. Wells Kara

Ella sat, waiting for my return. As I closed the door behind me, her eyes fluttered open. She gestured to the right, and we walked down a long, shadowy passage lit by candles and torches. "The Muse Urania is your last visit. If you have questions about the future or of things to come, she is the one who can guide and inspire you."

"And what of your future, Ella?"

"Not all of us journey the same way. I prefer being a guide. I am living my purpose as Priestess, Wayfinder, and Keeper of the Hall. Besides, the vacation package is outstanding." She laughed.

As we journeyed, a sense of elevation took hold. Time stretched, slowing to a crawl. My limbs moved as if through water, each step heavy, the atmosphere thick and charged. Invisible hands nudged me forward, urging me onward.

Ella grew lucent with brilliance, becoming a shining beacon in the darkness, lighting our way.

Corridors branched before us, one to the right, another to the left. Ella halted unexpectedly before an otherworldly door. Across the chamber, other passageways shimmered, each veiled in mystery.

"Why are so many of these gateways connected to the stars?"

"These lead to parallel timelines, each intertwined with this world. They are connected yet distinct. I will wait here as you complete this last Muse journey." She lifted her finger and wiped under her eyes.

"No goodbyes, Ella." A heavy ache settled in my chest as I wheeled the clear handle; a faint whisper called to me from the other side.

I met a frosty scene high on a faraway summit. My breath misted in the icy tundra chill. The sky swarmed with planets and stars. In the distance, near a row of pines, stood a quaint cottage with a river stone chimney. Smoke drifted upward, climbing into the evening sky. Making my way through several feet of snow toward the haven, I pressed my foot into the dense winter blanket, creating crunching sound beneath me. I zipped my jacket tighter and tucked my hands deep into my pockets. Silence surrounded me, and the wind was still, something was expanding within me.

Reaching the porch, I rang the bell, and the door swung open to a warm, inviting glow. Standing before me was Urania, the celestial Muse of the cosmos. Her starburst hazel eyes, flecked with green and blue, held a distant, entranced gaze. She was wrapped in a heavy midnight blue robe of stars and a golden belt cinched at her waist.

"Initiate, come in, I've already prepared the tea."

Inside, the space stretched far broader and deeper than the cottage's exterior. The walls were alive and ethereal. This place dwells between the worlds, defying the laws of space and time.

Urania walked to the far side of the room and opened the wide glass-panel doors. I followed her into a vast chamber where constellations floated within a domed glass ceiling. Across the room, a stargazing telescope pointed toward the stars. In the center, a stone pillar cradles a sacred chalice basin filled with water. Above it, a sparkling light thrumming in a steady, rhythmic pattern.

We made our way to the center. Urania lifted her hands over the basin.

"Open, as we invoke the rite of prophecy, purpose, and hope.

As we unveil the ancient messages of the cosmos, spoken by the prophetess who foretells what is to come. Receive the higher realms of creativity, truth, and love.

From the moment of birth, the signs and paths of destiny are set into motion. On the horizon, the soul slips through a portal into this existence. The planets, guided by the Heavens, chart the course for your ascent into the middle realm. Threaded by the Fates, a gift of earthly form and stardust yearning to merge with its true self.

You, born of the stars, live the dreams of mortal life and carry the memory of the Goddess. Awaken, now, the creative spark and bring it forth.

I, born of thunder and memory, carry the compass of the cosmic realm to steer humanity back to its heart, soul, and oneness."

She lowered her hands and bowed her head.

The Star & Sacred Fire

She filled our cups with steaming tea, her eyes twinkling. Leaning back in her plush chair, she took a sip. I was drawn to her, captivated by the stories she carried and what was to come.

"Initiate, my story is the oldest tale; it is one of visions, hope, dreams, and what is to come."

"I am not often viewed as a Muse in this world, except by adepts of astronomy or astrology. They are two distinct disciplines in your era but were once intertwined. They charted the planets, moon, and stars across the night sky, calculating and interpreting their influences.

In your world right now, Pluto is drifting into the waters of Aquarius, where it will remain for the next twenty years. This marks a new dawn. Collective energies are pouring in, and a renaissance is poised to shape the future—if humanity lets it form.

This moment brings me back to when the sacred fire was first gifted to humanity, the day I became the Muse of astronomy, astrology, and prophecy. It happened during a grand conjunction when the Sun embraced Pluto in perfect harmony with planets, stars, and celestial bodies you are yet to discover. But to speak of the future, we must first journey back to the day of my birth, thousands of years ago, before mortals had conceived of time or measure.

Part I – Great Shift on the Horizon

"As a child, I listened to the stars. I felt their longing, their dreams. They welcomed me, their patterns unfolding and revealing a great turning of what was yet to come. Mortals are not the only ones with visions, hopes, and dreams. These exist within all beings. We are all connected in this grand play of life, shaping worlds and universes. In time, humanity will come to see the bigger picture of existence."

She poured us another cup of tea.

"I'll share a story I've yet to speak aloud. A tale from the Second Great Turning, when mortals and Gods lost their way. A time when the Titan of creativity flourished and was revered. You may have heard his name: Prometheus.

Melete, Aoede, and Mneme were indeed the first Muses, but their Muse-like brother, Prometheus, made a significant contribution to the world. I shudder to imagine where all of us would be without him. I can still remember the final days when he visited our family on his way to Mount Olympus before he met his heroic and tragic fate."

Prometheus arrived during the late harvest with his brother, Epimetheus. They would offer an extra hand with the outdoor chores before winter took hold. Most evenings, Mother and Prometheus debated in lively conversation, discussing where each celestial resided. Their talks would end in laughter, acknowledging that there were so many Beings in our universe it was hard to remember them, even for Mneme.

I found Prometheus the gentlest and most compassionate of the Titans. He was sharp-witted, inventive, and wise, with patience and insight that far surpassed his brother's impulsive nature, especially during our family games.

One evening, at dusk, we sat side by side at a long table for our evening meal when someone mentioned Zeus. His name often, without fail, would find its way to the table. I often clenched my stomach.

"It is uncertain which resolution Zeus will take with the mortals, Klio. The Gods and Goddesses, in general, are displeased with how insipid mortals have become. I favor allowing them to find their own way. Some council members will meet with Zeus next week. You're welcome to join us. Mneme, your cooking is exceptional." Prometheus boasted and cheered.

Mother beamed.

He laughed as he reached for a glass, but it slipped and shattered. The pieces scattered across the floor. We both jumped to clear away the shards. He chuckled at the misstep, even as blood began to trickle from his finger. I reached for his hand, and in that moment, an unexpected vision overtook me.

Images and sounds filtered in and out as if I were submerged underwater. I could barely hold the sight of what was happening. Prometheus staggered at the base of a faraway mountain, battered, wounded, and exhausted. He cried out, "Urania before you is the most important and urgent of tasks…" *his voice dropped to a murmur.* "Take courage with you!" Then a golden light blinded my view.

"Urania, Urania, are you with us?" Polyhymnia helped me to my feet. As swift as the vision appeared, it receded.

"Fine, perhaps it was all the activities. Prometheus, are you okay?"

"It's a harmless scratch. I am sure one of the Muses will help me with the bandage. You should seek rest."

"I will walk you to your room," said Polyhynmia. A few paces out of view, she added. "Sister, you had that faraway look again."

I fell silent.

Once back inside my room I collapsed on the window seat. "I did have a vision of some sort, but I can't say for sure what it was trying to tell me."

"How long has this been happening?" asked Polyhymnia.

"For a while, I had intended to ask the Fates about it the last time they visited."

"What did it reveal to you about Prometheus?"

"How did you know?"

"When you grabbed his hand, you shifted. No one else noticed."

"Prometheus was wounded. He had an important task for me, but his words were mumbled. All I could make out was the word 'courage,' followed by a brilliant golden light."

Polyhymnia poked at the fire. "Urania, that's a lot to process. Sister, let me sit with this, and let's keep it between us for now. Let's not incite any anxiety.

I sense the council gathering will not go as Prometheus intends. I should check in on Klio and take my rest."

Wistfully gazing out the window, night covered the horizon as the Blood Star began to rise. I extended my senses, attuning to the frequency of his spirit. He spoke of a looming horizon where a war among the immortals would ensue unless its fierce flame was trusted to the one of Temperance. Leaders would fall into turmoil and division, and the future would be denied its birth. Something ancient pressed against my heart and knowing.

So, the Great Shift is upon us.

Part II – The Owl and the Serpent

I waved as Klio and Prometheus set out for Mount Olympus. "Don't worry, Klio has a plan in case things turn dire. They should reach the Olympian council in a day or two," Polyhymnia reassured me.

Though she told me not to worry, I paced the house for most of the day, trying to chart the season's changes. Anxiety shook my body. Something was amiss. Laying my head to rest, shadows crept through my sleep. I stood beneath a snowy peak, an unfamiliar, mysterious mountain. Prometheus was alive but struggling through bolts of lightning. In the darkness, a brilliant flaming sword. The dreamscape dissolved as a sharp knock jolted me awake.

"Urania, are you ok?" Polyhynmia asked.

"Yes, come in."

"Sister, you don't look well."

"I had another vision, mountain ranges laced with lightning. I do fear Prometheus is in harm's way."

"Sister, let us wait to hear the outcome before we take drastic action. We don't have enough information yet. These visions may be inflating things that might be a softer outcome. Let's get you outside and grounded. The garden needs some tending, and some breakfast will help."

After a light meal, we passed through the southern gate into a labyrinth of garden rooms and springs. Each wondrous space revealed its own unique blossoms and greenery, trailing for endless miles.

"I can see you have been busy, Polyhymnia."

"This is my sanctuary, though it requires constant tending. I am always grateful for the help. Why don't you start over there and pull up the bindweed."

I kneeled down and began to dig with a trowel. The Sun was welcoming, and the breeze carried a gentle coolness. We spent the entire afternoon tending by one of the Muse Springs. The area was abundant with life, drawing nearby frogs, deer, and other creatures. I felt more present than I had in months.

By early evening and weary from our tasks, I settled for a short rest. Out of the corner of my eye, a heart-shaped owl gilded with silence to a nearby willow tree. It perched with eyes fixed near the water. With a graceful leap, it swooped, grasping a black snake in its talons.

"No!" Polyhymnia cried. "Let's go, sister!"

Confused, I left my shoes as we dashed at full speed to the house. Storm clouds gathered, and flashes of lightning cracked in the direction of Mount Olympus.

Polyhymnia, out of breath, raised her voice. "Mother, Prometheus is in danger, and Klio may be in trouble."

Mneme paused to process. Hearing our distress, the other Muses appeared one by one on the veranda.

"Surely Zeus wouldn't punish his own daughter?"

We stared at Mother.

"Oh, of all the times the Fates are not here!" She said.

"Urania, can you gather enough strength to bring forth a vision?" asked Polyhymnia.

"I will try, perhaps, if you sing a chant to hasten the induction?"

She agreed. The family moved inside, and I rested on the floor as she invoked symbols with her hands, singing in a deep, ancient, primal tone. The other Muses joined in, amplifying the power and connection of the song.

"Urania, try to trace their location," Melpomene suggested.

As I relaxed, a sudden flood of warmth and sound jetted through my body, breaking me free from the physical. With accelerated speed, I lifted above the family and flew through the ceiling. I soared over rolling fields into the belly of storm-lit clouds. Mount Olympus towered ahead, and to the east were flames, plumes of smoke, and a terrain smoldering in ruin.

Skimming the treetops in a weightless sprint, I spotted Prometheus fleeing, defiant, desperate, outrunning Zeus's wrath. Bolts of lightning split the sky above him as he ran to the jagged peaks of an eastern mountain. I strained to keep pace, pushing forward with desperate force, but a fierce tug wrenched me back. In an instant, I was yanked back into the physical. Shaking, I breathed deeply and opened my eyes. My body ached. "Rough landing," I muttered."

Part III – Shifting Planets

"He's in the Caucasus Mountains," I said. "My vision faded before I reached the peaks, and I couldn't trace Klio's signature."

"To ensure Klio's safety, we created a backup plan. I spoke to her before she left. She sensed unease about the Olympians and went to document and lend her counsel," said Polyhymnia.

"Why didn't any of you tell me this?" Mother demanded, pacing with anxiety. "Why do you kids keep these things from me?"

The Muses burst into frantic voices, questions crashing over each other. Their words were desperate, seeking to know what to do next.

I raised my voice over the commotion. "I must be the one that goes."

A hush fell over the room, accompanied by blank expressions.

"In many of my visions, I am standing beside Prometheus. This is tied to the Great Turning we are about to encounter. Thalia and Terpsichore, you will stay with Mother."

"I should go with you, Urania; perhaps I can talk sense into Zeus!"

"That's not a wise action, Mother. It could cause more agitation." Polyhymnia said.

Mneme's brow furled.

"The rest will accompany me. We'll depart before the light breaks and search for Klio along the way."

My eyes were fixed on the candle flame. Unease gnawed at me. I stepped onto the balcony, restless, scanning the sky. The Storm Bringer squared the Blue Watcher, indicating a clash between rebellious forces, though it was hard to predict which way the power would go. Was this the right decision, and who is Temperance? Was it a mortal? Are they destined to save us all? Strangely, the question caused a calmness to flow over me.

Euterpe shook me awake. "It is time, sister."

Gathering my bag, I joined Euterpe and Polyhymnia in the hall. The rest of the family was waiting outside in front of the house.

"Euterpe and Polyhymnia will journey with me to the east. Melpomene, Calliope, and Erato will head north to locate Klio and bring her back. Sisters, we've never faced a situation like the Great Shift upon us. We're entering a time unlike any before. Mother, send for the Fates. We are going to need their guidance."

Calliope placed her foot in the stirrup and swiftly swung onto her horse, Kira. "Sister, what's the plan once you find Prometheus?"

"I trust the answers will come."

Part IV – Crown of Stars

I dipped my hand into the frigid waters at the farthest reaches of our known world. This shore marked the gateway to the east, where deep blue waters rolled beneath a wall of dark, jagged mountains rising in the distance.

Euterpe gathered kindling and sparked a fire for the evening. She took out her flute and began to play a soft and calming melody. Polyhymnia sang a soothing hymn. I paced to the cove in longing and fear, calling to the night-scape. The waters calmed, mirroring the heavens above.

A deep heartache opened me. What was to come of the world? I stood quietly in the darkness, holding onto my wishes for a benevolent outcome. Then a response came. A streak of light on the horizon crashed into the waves. From the dark sea, a luminous figure emerged, crowned with stars as bright as the sun. Her form, adorned with constellations, the embodiment of the night sky. The earth trembled as her words reverberated from the beginning of time.

"Urania, Muse, I felt your ache and longing. A vast precipice of change is elevating the world. Some mortals and Gods will falter, and some will become lost in the fluctuating tides. You and all the Muses must hold fast to the sacred flame of creation. It is yours to ignite humanity, to guide, and to kindle the way through the confusion. Your meeting with Prometheus has to come to pass, but his fate is not in your hands. The task he will give you is yours alone." Her words hung in the air, heavy with destiny.

The Goddess opened her hand to present a miniature model of the cosmos, spinning and unfolding.

"The world is on the cusp of a rebirth. In this transition, many things will fall away. Each soul must choose how they will navigate this shift. We, the Stars, are here to nurture you and reveal the possibilities for what is to come."

The Goddess reached for one of the radiant stars in her crown and placed it upon my brow. A light expanded within my inner sight. My fears melted as my mind quieted and emptied, ready for the wisdom of the cosmos.

"Urania, Muse of the heavens, I bless upon you this celestial wisdom of the sacred patterns and creative fire. That which weaves through life, the cosmos, and consciousness. Make clear and open the way for the new beginning."

Part V – Torch of the Sacred Flame

"Then she disappeared," I explained to Euterpe and Polyhymnia.

"So we can't help Prometheus?" inquired Euterpe.

"It is not in our hands," I said.

"I need a minute." Euterpe dropped her things and walked to the water's edge, folding her arms.

Polyhymnia drank her special herbal brew, then searched the plain. "The Caucasus Mountains are close. I can sense it. Beyond that direction is the western gate."

"We don't have much time," I stated.

As we passed through towering clay-engraved columns on each side of us, I was drawn to the eerie peaks capped with snow. "We are in the right place. This is exactly like my vision."

Euterpe gulped, "It's quiet, creepy quiet."

"The skies are too clear, and the sun overhead casts no shadows," Polyhynmia added.

Euterpe raised her flute and played a bright, high tone. Within minutes, several crows flew from behind us and circled overhead. She played a few more notes, and they swooped down, landing in a circle around us.

One perched on her arm, "caw-caw."

"Please guide the way to Prometheus," Euterpe asked.

We followed their swift flight toward the highest peak. Polyhymnia spoke and spun a circle of protection around us.

The crows landed at the base of the mountain, pecking through the thick snow. Euterpe studied the path. "The footsteps and blood go this way. We're close," she said, placing her flute to her lips and playing a few notes. We watched the crows take flight and leave southward.

The mountain towered twice as high as Parnassus, and its snowdrifts were three times as deep. With each stride, the winds grew fiercer. Halfway to the summit, we found a cave, its entrance a refuge from the relentless weather.

Polyhumnia pointed, "Let's regroup and take cover. We need a plan."

The cave was dark. Polyhymnia spelled a fire, bringing it to life. At the back of the cave, several torches and two tunnels branched off in opposite directions. Euterpe secured one of the torches and sifted through bones.

"Whatever was here, let's hope it doesn't return," Euterpe said, her voice low. "What's the plan once we find Prometheus? Are we bringing him back to Mother's house?"

"He must go to the Fates, where he will be kept shielded and far from Mount Olympus," Polyhymnia said. "Perhaps Zeus will forget about this matter."

"I am not going anywhere!"

Startled, we all turned.

"By the Gods, Prometheus!" I dropped my things and rushed over. Prometheus braced himself at the entrance of one of the tunnels. Though in pain, he managed a faint smile.

Polyhymnia leaped forward, "Hold on." She caught his arm and gently lowered him to the ground to inspect his wounds. Across his back and chest, red branch-like burns marked his skin, clearly from a bolt of lightning.

"I will regenerate, but it will take time," he said. "I was waiting until I could make my way back to Mount Olympus."

"Why would you go back to Zeus?" Euterpe threw up her hands.

"Have you seen Klio? Is she okay?" I asked.

"Yes, I trust she is okay. She is a cunning one," said Prometheus.

I studied the situation and whispered to Polyhymnia. "How long will his wounds take to heal?"

"Weeks," Polyhymnia gestured.

Prometheus, sweating in his delirium, continued. "He plans to erase the mortals. I seek to challenge Zeus's decision! Many of the Gods are divided on what to do. Some want to grant mortals autonomy. We tried negotiating."

Euterpe threw more sticks on the fire, "Why would Zeus do such a thing?!"

This is the Great Turning, the era the Star Goddess had warned me about. We have to pick sides and battles. I hope Temperance delivers us from this mounting war, I thought.

"At the second meeting, I argued for mortals so they may enhance and empower their lives. Despite all my efforts and the support of the Goddesses who spoke, it did not steer his decision. Zeus grew restless, dismissing us, then proclaiming a decree: If the mortals do not submit their allegiance to me and cease their rebellion in the year, they will be wiped out! He told the council to meet in one year."

Polyhymnia took a deep breath, centering herself. "This is far more serious than I thought."

Prometheus chuckled. "All is not lost, Muses. When the council adjourned, I enlisted Klio and Athena to keep Zeus distracted with other civic matters of state. As they did, I slipped away, running through the garden, past the guards, and into the great chamber of light. Within those walls burns the most powerful sacred fire. A flame ignited by the dawn of creation, older than even the Gods and Goddesses. I took a fennel stick, captured the sacred fire within it, and rejoined the gathering without a God noticing."

"Klio was waiting for me at the southern road, but as I approached the final gate of the temple, Zeus's guards ambushed me. I fought my way free, sprinting and leaping over the walls. When I glimpsed back, Klio had run into the shadows."

"Zeus unleashed a storm of fury and lightning. I outran his wrath, but one of his thunderbolts struck me. Barely escaping, I made my way here. A place where Zeus treads lightly. The creatures of this area will challenge him."

Polyhmnia pressed a cloth drenched in herbs over his wounds. He winced, his breath coming in sharp gasps. "It will take time to heal, Prometheus. Save your strength."

"We must take him to the Fates," said Euterpe.

Polyhynmia held out her hand to quiet us.

"Poorrtmeetthhus!"

Euterpe dashed toward the cave entrance.

"Prometheus! We know you are in the mountains!"

It's Zeus, I recognize his cadence and condescending attitude," Prometheus said.

Euterpe snuffed out the torch and crawled closer to the entrance for a better view. "He is with reinforcements!"

Prometheus reached out. "Urania! Before you, a most heavy and urgent task. Bring me one of the torches!"

I sprinted to the back of the cave, but a sharp crack split the air. A brilliant flash of golden light flooded the cave, blinding us. From the mist emerged a goddess in bright golden armor wielding a flaming sword.

"Prometheus, I figured I would find you in the Caucasus!"

"ATHENA!" He struggled to rise.

"What chaos did you get yourself into?" She knelt to check his wound and wore a sense of worry.

"Hard to fight lightning," he chuckled.

"I heard about the fire, Prometheus. We're fortunate the Muses stand with you. But time is short. I'm going to offer you the only option. I will turn you in. There is nowhere you can hide from Zeus. He will tear the worlds apart, hunting you down. Several members of the council and I will negotiate with him on your behalf. If he refuses, we will find a way to free you. Muse, bring over the torch."

Prometheus, with trembling and scorched hands, reached into his bag and drew out the fennel stalk. With solemn grace and trust, he gave it to Athena.

Athena extended the flame to me. "By the Goddess, this sacred fire is entrusted to you, Urania, to deliver to humanity for their survival and empowerment. Swear me your oath; You will unite this flame within every Muse and safeguard it! This fire is a gift for humanity's creativity and rebirth. It is to be held sacred, honored, and cultivated."

I extended the torch. "I give you my oath, Athena, with Prometheus and my sisters as witnesses!"

As the fire ignited the torch, a crackling beam of light swept through the cave, soaring upward. Threads of molten gold, a radiant tapestry flew between the fennel stick and torch. The star on my brow from the Goddess's crown merged with the sacred fire, flooding my eyes with illumination.

Athena drew out another reed and captured a portion of the fire. One more spectacle of light bounced off the walls. She tucked the flame carefully into her armor. "I will give this fire to those ready for its power. The sacred fire is never to rest in the hands of a single Being!"

Prometheus lifted his head, "Take courage with you, Urania! You must pass the flame to Temperance."

"Who is Temperance?"

Athena knelt and extended her arms beneath Prometheus. "We must move quickly."

"Wait!" Polyhymnia called out. "This will ease his pain and keep Zeus from harming him. He will be unresponsive for many weeks. It will give you time." She traced symbols and spoke soft notes that vibrated through his body. Prometheus closed his eyes and slipped into an unconscious state.

"Muse, I owe you," Athena said. "Now, go! Take the cave to the right. It will lead you north and back home. Kilo has already met with your sisters. Zeus will remain unaware of our meeting."

With that, Athena gently secured Prometheus' limp form and carried him back through the cave entrance.

I held the flaming torch close. "This way, sisters."

Part VI – Rebirth of the Muses

Ten of us stood in a circle beneath the first full moon of spring. We had journeyed covertly along the coastline and safely returned home. The Divine flame was placed in an unassuming lantern, sealed with a spell of protection. The *torch* became an emblem of the ritual of rebirth, just like the *Well of Creation*, both serving as potent symbols of our Muse's sacred power.

I held the original torch and reignited it with the sacred fire.

"By the Gods and Goddesses of the sacred fire and Source, we vow to carry and inspire the spark in all mortals for their well-being and survival so they may grow and thrive. We pass on the sacred light of creativity, inspiration, passion, and awakening for the love of all Beings. From this night forward, we inspire, ignite, and rebirth the world's vision anew."

Circling the central fire, I passed the flame from one Muse to the next. The sacred fire streamed and united into each of them, awakening and amplifying their unique gifts. One by one, each Muse stepped forward.

Mneme was first:
"I, Mneme, raise this torch so humanity never forgets!"

Klio followed:
"I, Klio, raise this torch as keeper of the past to inspire with wisdom and what came before!"

Melpomene stepped forward:
"I, Melpomene, raise this torch of living and liberation!"

Next, Erato:
"I, Erato, raise this torch of desire, erotic poetry, and ecstasy of the wild heart!"

Euterpe moved in:
"I, Euterpe, raise this torch of music and expression!"

Terpsichore with a fluid gesture:
"I, Terpsichore, raise this torch with the embodiment of the cosmic dance and freedom!"

Thalia jumped forward:
"I, Thalia, raise this torch of joy and laughter, bringer of spring and play!"

Calliope moved close:

"I, Calliope, raise this torch of the storyteller, the eloquent voice, and epic poetry!"

Polyhymnia stepped in and held the torch as high as she could:
"I, Polyhymnia, raise this torch and sing the hymn of sacred union, truth, and devotion!"

As the future, I moved closer:
"I, Urania, raise this torch of the prophetess, wisdom keeper of the sacred patterns and movement of the stars!"

With our torches held high, we watched as the smoke and energy soared into the atmosphere, carrying our inspiration on the winds across the world—for those ready for the fire to ignite their creative heart.

Finally, I reached out and placed two more torches in the circle, symbols for Muses yet to be.

We begin…

Eleven Muses

In the beginning, there were three
Titans of magic, Beings of Light
who sang to the world
and remembered its beauty

Then, nine were birthed
born of Memory and Thunder
who held the gifts and dreams
of a changing world

Next Prometheus
who delivered the sacred spark
to renew humanity and the world
for them to carry their inner power

In turn, the world flourished
building, innovating, designing
civilizations grew and thrived
expanding life and expression

In the future, two more torches
emerging from the depths
waiting to be born and written
Muses soon to be

Journey to the Stars & Future

"Here is one last journey, Initiate. We will travel to the stars and the future." Urania settles into her chair.

Find a comfortable position, close your eyes, and bring your attention to your body. Take a few deep, steady breaths, allowing yourself to relax. Feel the surface beneath you supporting you as you settle in and release tension. With each breath, sense yourself becoming lighter, as if gravity is loosening its hold. A soft lightness rises through your body. Imagine gently lifting upward into the clear blue sky. The sun's warm rays wash over you. Notice how the colors shift from soft blues to deeper hues of indigo and violet as you ascend.

Continue upward and sense the vastness around you. Stars begin to emerge, shimmering in every direction. Below, Gaea moves in harmony, alive, luminous, and steady on her path through the cosmos.

Drift farther into space. Ahead of you, starlight gathers and builds. A figure begins to take form, radiant, serene, woven from the stars themselves. The figure becomes more defined, appearing before you as the Star Goddess.

She greets you with warmth and unconditional love and gestures toward the vast, boundless universe. As you look, you witness stars colliding, planets forming, and galaxies spiraling outward into the unknown.

The Goddess speaks: "A Divine plan is set in motion. At this crossroads, there are many possible timelines, and we all play a part in how it unfolds. It is malleable, shaped by how ready humanity is for its evolution."

The Star Goddess turns to you and presents you with three gifts, one by one, each to guide you on your journey in the months and years ahead. Take your time. Let questions arise to ask her. (Pause)

When you feel complete, let her insights settle within you. Offer your gratitude to the Star Goddess for her presence and guidance. (Pause)

As you begin to return to Gaea, notice a radiant white and gold light enveloping the entire planet. See it…feel it…as it flows into every corner of the world, embracing all beings. (Pause)

The Star Goddess tells you in her soft voice: "This is where humanity is heading. It may not seem so now, but these are the currents of love and creativity, destined to unfold in ways beyond imagination."

You watch as this powerful light continues to expand, covering not only the Earth but streaming out beyond galaxies.

It's time to return. Bring with you the three gifts and Gaea's healing energy, love, and abundance. Keep them close to your heart.

Say your farewells and offer your thanks. As you do, the Goddess dissolves into starlight, and you feel a gentle pull guiding you back. Drifting through the sky, you return down slowly, peacefully, to your body, to the room where you sit or lie. When you are ready, open your eyes.

Well-Wish from Urania

"Stand with me by this sacred well, Initiate. Allow me to place this final well-wish upon you. Rest now; the future is already unfolding. The planets and stars shine their love upon you, guiding your way. You are the flame and the longing of creation itself."

Allow things to fall away
Allow yourself a thriving life
Allow the stars to speak and guide you
Allow inspiration to move you
Allow yourself to be your purpose
Allow the creative self to emerge
Allow and trust in what is to come
Allow yourself to be reborn
Again and again…

Sit with me by the moonlight
I am dreaming of you there
May my love carry you to the future
of who you already are.

With reverence and love,
Urania

Chapter XIV
Closing Ritual: Choose Your Own Adventure

"The Muses bless those who dare to create." —Hesiod

I FOUND MYSELF BACK IN THE HALL, WHERE ELLA STOOD WAITING IN FULL REGALIA. Well done, Initiate, you made it! Congratulations!" she said, clapping. "You are now self-initiated by the Muses. From here, you're presented with choices for how you wish to journey forward."

"Their stories, rituals, and creations have already begun to shift you in subtle ways. One morning, you'll awaken and notice a change. It might show up in how you connect, create, or approach life itself."

"As you move beyond this container, give yourself time to integrate into your rebirth. You may choose to work more closely with one or several of the Muses, or you might feel called to a different path entirely."

Ella took out an ancient key and turned it, unlocking the door to another Hall. "Let us end as we began. I've brought you to the final set of doors. Here, you will choose and enter one of these three thresholds."

"The first is to continue with the Muses, working with one or more of them for a set period, moving deeper into the mysteries. You may choose to connect with them regularly, continuing your relationship to inspire your work and guide your creative journey."

"The second is an inner path, an invitation to meet a guide who will become your personal Muse and spiritual mentor. Perhaps someone who already inspires you, or maybe someone unexpected will appear. This is a path you will walk alone."

"The third is the path of departure from the Muses, this Hall, and the magic itself. You've received what you need and are ready to complete your journey. Know that you are always welcome to return."

"Dear Initiate, this is where our paths conclude," Ella said, her voice warm. "I've truly enjoyed our time together. It's been a pleasure to guide and support you on this path."

"I'll miss you, Ella. You've taken me so far on this journey, and I'm not great with goodbyes."

Ella hugged me close. "Grace, I know which door you'll choose."

With that, she touched the brim of her hat and vanished.

Take a breath, dear reader, *Initiate*, and choose a door.

Acknowledgments

This book would not have come to life without the guidance, encouragement, and support of many extraordinary individuals. To consulting editor Cheri M. Hyde, whose insights helped refine my vision, thank you for your valuable time and support. A special thanks to Jamie Smith, Megan Fresh, Teri Pierson, and Colette Gardiner for their feedback and unwavering belief in this project, as well as to my readers, who continue to support and inspire me. Last, I wish to acknowledge the Muses and ancient voices whose influence and inspiration continue to shape my understanding of myth, healing, and storytelling.

Bibliography

Hesiod. *Theogony.* Translated by M. L. West. Revised reissue. Oxford: Oxford University Press, 2009.

Podlecki, Anthony J. *The Early Greek Poets and Their Times.* Vancouver: University of British Columbia Press, 1984.

Plutarch. *Septem Sapientium Convivium.* Vol. II. Loeb Classical Library Edition, 1928.

Rosen, Ralph M., and Susan H. Rosen. *Arts & Humanities Through the Eras: Ancient Greece and Rome (1200 B.C.E.–476 C.E.).* Gale Research Inc., 2004.

Russell, Eugenia. *Literature and Culture in Late Byzantine Thessalonica.* 1st ed. London: Bloomsbury Publishing Plc, 2014.

About the Author

J. Wells Kara is a debut author, artist, and spiritual guide who has spent over a decade exploring the transformative power of mystery school teachings and the magical arts. Through her journey, she has immersed herself in sacred rituals, channeling, divination, and alchemical healing—each experience leading to profound personal growth. Now, she's passionate about helping others reconnect with their authentic selves, guiding them on their own path of rebirth and self-realization. Her work encourages readers to embrace their inner truths, awaken their creative potential, and live in alignment with their highest selves. Known for its depth and transformative impact, her writing inspires those ready to tap into the infinite power within. With a background in architecture and a black belt in Aikido, J. Wells Kara blends artistic vision, spiritual practice, and embodied wisdom to create a life of balance and purpose. Discover more at www.jwellskara.com